Prime Rib & Apple

Jill Briscoe

ZONDERVAN
PUBLISHING HOUSE
OF THE ZONDERVAN CORPORATION
GRAND RAPIQS, MICHIGAN 49506

PRIME RIB AND APPLE
© 1976 by The Zondervan Corporation
Grand Rapids, Michigan

Fifth printing   October 1978

Library of Congress Cataloging in Publication Data

Briscoe, Jill.
    Prime Rib and Apple.

    1. Women in the Bible.   I. Title.
BS575.B 67   220.8'30141'2   76-25054

Printed in the United States of America

To Peggy
the most loving and giving mother
the Lord ever gave to a girl, I gratefully
dedicate this book

Contents

Foreword

In recent years, my life has been blessed by Jill Briscoe's magnetic witness and by her gifts to me of herself, her abiding faith in the Lord Jesus Christ, and her understanding that in God's Word lie sure guidelines that can lead one safely through the difficult and demanding journey of modern living.

My experience has not been unique, for hundreds of women who have learned to know Jill through the Bible classes she teaches in her home city agree with me about the impact of her ministry.

Now, through *Prime Rib and Apple*, countless others will be blessed by all that she has to offer. I love this book, for it is laced with Jill's humor and imagination, and it is rich with her deep insights into the vital, practical, everyday lessons to be learned from Scripture. I suspect that the Spirit of God has been saving *Prime Rib and Apple* for this day and this hour.

MILLIE DIENERT

Preface

Women of the Bible. Ugh! What a hackneyed and overused title! When I began to write a book on this subject, I said to Omnipotence, "Please give me some new insights into the little man-esses who skip through Your book. Something new, something I've never seen before. Something fresh and something creative." He gave me *Prime Rib and Apple,* and I've enjoyed every minute of meeting Ribs I had never really understood before.

I see myself in every one — in Sarah, Lot's wife, Hannah, and *especially* in Dripping Tap (I didn't enjoy meeting her one little bit; it was too much like looking in the mirror!). I've discovered anew that Omnipotence loved them all — and if them, then me, too! With all our weaknesses, His strength is sufficient. Remember, Omnipotence is love, truth, power. And I love Him dearly for all that *He is* in the midst of all that *I am not!*

"Most gladly therefore will I rather glory in my infirmities, that the power of Christ may rest upon me. . . . for when I am weak, then am I strong" (2 Cor. 12:9, 10).

> *Omnipotence will keep me,*
> *Omnipotence will change me,*
> *For Omnipotence is Omnipotence,*
> *And Omnipotence is mine!*

Prime Rib and Apple

Eve

Prime Rib snuggled down happily inside her rib cage. It was warm, cozy, and dark inside Adam, and all the other ribs were fast asleep. Even though Prime Rib had no light by which to judge the lateness of the hour, somehow she knew Adam should have been up and about his work long ago. She moved slowly, very slowly, up and down, as his heart beat rhythmically. He seemed to be *very* asleep, she thought. She liked being so near Adam's heart. Somehow it felt just right. She was where she was "made" to be, and that had to be *very good.*

Suddenly the world seemed to spin. There was a deafening noise, as the flesh above her was severed. Prime Rib screamed, and all the other little ribs in the cage woke up. For the first time in her life she saw the blue sky, although she didn't know what it was, of course.

Then she saw Him. *Omnipotence.* He was smiling at her in the strangest sort of way. "Prime Rib," He said ever so gently, "I have chosen you for a special task. I want you to help Adam."

"How?" she whispered.

"Well now, you've been a help already," He said, "but you would be even more of a blessing to Adam *outside* his body. Have you noticed you're in a cage down there? Wouldn't you like to be free?"

"Free? Outside? What's that?" she gasped.

"Well," He said patiently, "you are 'there,' and 'there' is inside. I am 'here,' and 'here' is outside."

"Well," thought Prime Rib, "if there is an outside with Omnipotence, that *has* to be better!"

"I'm going to take you gently between my thumb and forefinger, little Rib, break you away from your man's heart, change your structure by giving you a body like his, and breathe upon you so you may become a living soul."

"But what will be the purpose of my existence outside of Adam?" Prime Rib cried. "I'll die! Severed from him I'll simply feel like a useless 'spare rib'! I don't know if I want to get out of my cage."

"You'll be free to get right back where you belong," explained Omnipotence. "Who said anything about your being independent? You will have more of a 'prime' function than before. You will surely bring more joy to Adam as you yield and respond to him of your own glad will than you could as a mere piece of bone without the power of choice! Adam will be conscious of something missing — and it will be *you*, his Prime Rib! When I bring you together again, you will both be complete. And you will both be satisfied. Will you come?"

Prime Rib thought long and hard. To be to Adam more than she was now? Why, now she was part of his very being. But she decided to entrust herself to His will and purpose. "Take me, Omnipotence," she began. Her words

16

were lost as He laughed out loud, and Prime Rib thought she'd never in her life heard anything as delightful as that sound — it filled the universe. Omnipotence cupped the little Rib in His hand and breathed upon her and glory filled her soul! It was finished. She was a man-ess. And the Lord God closed up Adam's flesh and brought her to the man, and the man said,

> "This is now bone of my bones,
>   and flesh of my flesh:
> She shall be called Woman,
>   because she was taken out of Man" (Gen. 2:23).

Prime Rib was somewhat confused. She had become so many things in such a short time! She still remembered her humble origin. At the same time, balanced unsteadily on her new feet, she contemplated the fact that she was now like the man she loved. She was like Adam. She was a man-ess. Even as this thought ensued, a greater fact presented itself to her new mind — the fact that she was now like Him — Omnipotence. After His image.

Eternal was her soul, responsible must be her actions, free-willing her spirit toward His commands. She had become a personal, rational, moral being, free forever to choose to fit back into Adam's life.

Omnipotence smiled. He saw that it was all very, very good.

> A handful of dust in the hand of Omnipotence,
>   the warm breath of God giving life to the soul,
> A piece of dry bone to help meet his Onlyness —
>   Yes, God made a man-ess and Adam was whole!

Now I don't know if you believe all that or not. That's how it was, the Bible says, and I believe it. If Omnipotence *is* Omnipotence, no problem! He can make a man or a woman out of anything — a stone, a worm, even a piece of cake! It doesn't really matter. I'm just glad He used a handful of dust and an old dry bone, because it reminds us not to get too uppity. The staggering thing is — the man and man-ess *did* get uppity. Can you imagine?

They pulled the plug! They had been plugged into the direct current from heaven. Then one day that stupid little piece of bone, with all the undeserved blessings of a free will entrusted to her by the almighty Godhead, blew the fuse!

She reckoned (quite wrongly) in her small man-ess brain that she had simply escaped from one cage into another. This time she was in the cage of "expected obedience." Certainly it was larger, but did that mean it was any better? A terrible thought was presented to Prime Rib, and because she had never had a terrible thought before, she didn't recognize how terrible it was! It was quite different from the thoughts she was used to having, but just because it was different didn't necessarily mean it was *wrong*, did it?

The Snake assured her it didn't! Since he was the source of the terrible thought, he was busy dressing it up like a flower and making it smell sweet.

"Why shouldn't you escape and be your own person?" he inquired. "After all, that was what Omnipotence had in mind in the first place, wasn't it? Didn't He say He would make you like Him? Well, He was His own God and did His own thing; surely if you did the same it would please Him! Why should you plug up the hole in Adam's heart? What about *your* heart?" he hissed. "Why waste time worrying about *his* needs. What about *your* needs?" he continued.

Prime Rib lay very still. Creation quieted, listening for her answer.

The Snake peered suspiciously over his shoulder (which really hurt, as a snake's shoulder sort of goes right on down to the tip of his tail). He was trying to see what Jesus was doing. He knew the Second Person of the Trinity was listening for Prime Rib's response, as he'd seen Him watching closely from the portals of heaven. "Whatever is He up to?" mused the Snake. It looked as if He was getting ready for a journey! Where would He be going?

Abruptly the Snake returned to the scene of his crime. Nestling close to Prime Rib's ear, he suggested she liberate Adam as well as herself. "Didn't Omnipotence tell you to help your man? Well, help him to begin a new relationship. Help him to grow up and depend on himself instead of you. Show him he needs to be his own man. You can do it! Have an apple," he ended, subsiding into a pile of leaves. If the Snake could have prayed for the success of his plot, he would have done so, but, of course, he couldn't. He was now totally dependent upon himself, so it was no use asking for help! He was so lost he didn't even want to help himself! All he desired were the souls of Adam and Eve, food for him in the hell he had instituted — the hell of his rebellion against his Creator.

Prime Rib took the hand Omnipotence had fashioned from her little piece of bone and plucked the piece of forbidden fruit. She placed it between the lips Omnipotence had framed to praise Him and absorbed into her system the poisons of independence, selfishness, and *death*. And Jesus prepared to leave for Bethlehem.

"Oh, the power of a Rib," the Snake shrieked.

A lion sprang upon a lamb and tore it to bloody shreds. Two beautiful elk locked horns in mortal combat. A cat began to play with a mouse. And Eve went to find Adam. The angels were appalled! Surely Adam would refuse the fruit. After all, Adam was so strong. Look at all he had going for him. Surely Prime Rib would be rebuked and rejected.

Omnipotence sighed. He knew what Adam was about to do. He'd known all along. And yet knowing, He still took His little piece of bone from His handful of dust and gave them the dignity of personhood and freedom. Knowing their rejection, He planned for their redemption.

Omnipotence *could* do it. Omnipotence *would* do it. Because He *is Omnipotence* and *Omnipotence is Love!*

Now Love began to ask eternal questions: "Where are you? What have you done? Who told you that you were naked? Did you disobey?" And Adam said, "Prime Rib made me do it." And Prime Rib said, "The Snake made me do it." And Love said, "You *both* did it, and now it's *done!* You chose to choose, and choosing chose to die!"

Omnipotence turned His holy wrath upon Lucifer, Son of the Morning, who had become the Snake, Father of the Night. "Upon thy belly shalt thou go, and dust shalt thou eat all the days of thy life," He said (Gen. 3:14).

The Snake cursed Love whose curse he bore and thought of all of us. He had reached the man through Prime Rib once; he would do it again and again. His anger at the frustration of his purpose knew no bounds. His devices would not, could not change.

Nor need they! He laughed and listened to Omnipotence placing Prime Rib under Adam's headship. The Snake knew how right He was. Prime Rib needed a head! Oh, the power of that little piece of bone. Powerless over the Snake maybe, but powerful enough to poison Adam. What he had not been able to do, she had been able to accomplish nicely without him. So it would be in ensuing generations!

The little man-ess wept bitter tears of repentance, and Omnipotence took His heavenly handkerchief, which He reserves in glory to wipe away all tears from all faces, and comforted her.

20

"Where did I go wrong, Omnipotence?" she asked. "Why did I listen to him? How did he beguile me so easily?"

Omnipotence explained how the Snake examines our lives for potential weaknesses and, having watched us carefully, approaches, attacks, and if allowed to engage us in debate, finally achieves his black results. "He watched you, Prime Rib, and saw three potential trouble spots in your character, and these he used!"

"What were they?" the little broken bone inquired.

"A Prime Rib loves to talk," Omnipotence explained. "Now, I invented words, and they're a great idea as long as you don't overdo it! I thought of them so I could communicate with you. But you can't talk and listen at the same time, and therein lies the danger. I could see you'd never hear my warnings when all that noise was coming out of you! Talk, talk, talk! If it wasn't Adam, it was the animals. Didn't you notice the giraffe's neck was getting longer and longer trying to get out of earshot? You should have been warned when the elephant's flaps started to lie protectively over the holes in his head, instead of standing upright as I created them! You'd been bending his ear, Prime Rib.

"How easy it was for the evil one's spirit to enter into one of your favorite animals and attract your attention. Even he found it difficult to get a word in edgewise, but when he did, you listened carelessly, not recognizing who it was that spoke to you. His subtlety is such that he would speak through such a lovely friend!"

"I tried to argue," Prime Rib began.

Omnipotence sternly answered, "My angels dare not argue with nor rebuke the Snake. Then how do you suppose you can overcome? You should have refused to converse, rejected his proposals, and referred him to Me. You are no match alone."

"What else did I do wrong?" the man-ess asked.

"You wanted too much," Omnipotence replied.

"I had so much," Prime Rib exclaimed. "Why did I long for more?"

"The Snake composed a tune to which you eventually danced," Omnipotence answered. "It was this: 'Paradise isn't enough. Paradise isn't the best. You can have more than enough, but only I am offering you that!' To want more than I provide is to want too much. The 'too much' only the Snake can offer you is the 'too much' of stepping out of the role for which you have been created. I made you a man-ess, not a goddess! I created you to cleave, not leave! I made the woman for the man, not the man for the woman. That is the truth. Yet you believed a lie.

"And then, you ate too much," Omnipotence continued. "I made you able to feel hungry, but I made you able to stay hungry, too. The Snake will tell you that a bite of disobedience will stay your hunger. That is a lie. My Son will come to know the hunger of obedience. When offered bread, He'll choose to starve, for My good will shall His meat be. It should have been sufficient, too, for thee!"

"It looked so tasty," Prime Rib whispered. "But, oh, how sick I am!"

"The Snake isn't stupid," Omnipotence replied. "He will not offer you a rotten apple, but beautiful though it be, you should refuse, and in the doing find your satisfaction."

Prime Rib wept for spoiled creation and the beasts, but most of all, she wept for Adam. Omnipotence looked down the years and wept for her. He thought of Cain, the world's first murderer, of Abel's spilled blood, and of Prime Rib's broken heart.

Then lifting his little man and man-ess into His ever-lasting arms, He showed them the end times when the Snake would be forever chained in darkness. "Pray for your offspring, little dust-and-bone people," He commanded. "Pray hard, pray long, and tell them your story. But don't forget in the telling to tell them Mine as well. Do you remember what it is?

"Knowing your rejection, I've planned for your redemption!"

And the Prime Rib said,

> *Omnipotence can do it,*
> *Omnipotence will do it,*
> *For Omnipotence is Omnipotence,*
> *And Omnipotence is love!*

WHY?

Omnipotence, why did You make mankind *first*
When knowledge included their sinning?
Then all of Your effort creating the world
Could have ceased at the very beginning.
Why didn't You let us all hang there in space?
Why spoil it for four-legged creatures?
Why mar Your pure image entrusted to man
And stamped on his spiritual features?
Why did Your great power create for us light,
When darkness would suit our rejection?
Why plan for us food and delights for the sight?
Why bother with angel protection?
Why didn't the animals tear us to pieces?
Why didn't the fish drown us all?
Why didn't the flowers just strangle and choke us?
Who stopped them from growing so tall?

Prime Rib and Apple

Why did You let the cursed earth go on giving,
Despite all our wars and pollution?
Why balance the oxygen nicely for living,
For man to scream out "revolution"?
Why enter at all Your cursed creation?
Why need You a promise to make?
Why risk extinction at Your own incarnation?
Why be nailed to the cross for my sake?
Why holes in Your palms and Your back lacerated?
Why whipping and spitting and hate?
Why throw the cross down
Till Your bones dislocated?
Did You leave Your escape route too late?
What were Your thoughts when Your Spirit departed
And You spent those three black days in hell?
Did You remember Genesis One
And Your world when You made all things well?
Why did You bother to let us all know
When You triumphed and rose from the dead?
Why didn't You just take a ticket to heaven
When no one believed what You said?
Oh, why did You bother to make a new Eden
For Adams and Eves like us all?

Omnipotence loved us — the facts tell the tale,
His death paid the price for our fall.

When to Disobey Your Husband
Sarah

Contention was lonely. Contention always is. No one wants to compete with her because she always has to win. Contention lost all her friends. Contention always does. Those picky little things aren't worth a war anyway! Contention answers back, "Why should I? How dare you? You hurt me!" Contention stamps her foot and lies to save her skin. Contention is not very beautiful after all.

"But, is anything too hard for the Lord?" Contention can be changed. A common beauty can a princess be!

Omnipotence could do it,
Omnipotence would do it,
Because Omnipotence is Omnipotence,
And Omnipotence is *power!*

Contention was married to Abram, who thought she was extremely beautiful. And so she was — on the outside! If only her character could match up. She had not been named Contention for nothing!

27

Omnipotence carefully observed Abram's deliberations as he traversed the path home. The man was seeking a way to break his news to his wife. Suddenly the patriarch changed direction and headed for downtown Haran. Heaven tuned in to the interesting conversation ensuing between Abram and the merchant Jacob.

"I need to buy your biggest and best tent."

"A tent?"

"A tent! You heard me, good Jacob. Now are you or are you not in real estate?" Abram smiled evenly, mischievously enjoying Jacob's confusion.

"Sir, of course, of course. A tent you shall have. My biggest and best!"

Where is the patriarch building? Jacob wondered. *When is it all going to begin, and what is the tent for? Maybe it is for the workers as they build an addition to the mansion.* He busied himself selecting the list of goods his customer demanded, while Abram watched him quietly, wondering just what he was going to say. He knew the question had to come, and come it did.

"Excuse my asking, sir, but I trust you're not moving back to Ur of the Chaldees. We wouldn't want you to leave Haran just now."

Abram sighed, then smiling wryly he sought to give an answer he didn't have! "Jacob, we will be leaving Haran in a little while," he began. "I can tell you we won't be going back to Ur, but I can't tell you just where we will be heading. Toward the Negev probably."

Jacob's mind searched frantically for some solid ground of reasonableness. The Negev was the arid desert wilderness! An incredible mental picture of Sarai casually hanging her chandelier from the tent pole, sunning herself by a muddy desert pool, and swatting flies with her palm frond flitted across his mind!

He was not alone in his imaginings. Abram, too, was thinking of his wife. What would he say when Contention began asking questions? "Where, Abram?" she would ask, the audacity of her beauty shattering his determined course. He wouldn't answer because he didn't know; he didn't know because he hadn't heard; he hadn't heard because one never does hear. You see, if God tells you to do something, He waits for you to obey. He's not about to tell the next step until the first is taken, and Abram had not yet taken the first!

"Get thee out of thy country, and from thy kindred, and from thy father's house," Omnipotence had said. How much time had passed since He had said it we do not know, but we know it had been said; and we also know it had not been done.

Possibly it had not been done because the next step had not been revealed. Maybe "unto a land that I will shew thee" had not been sufficiently explicit. Perhaps Abram was waiting for the book to be written before he traversed page one. But that is not God's way either. A command is a command and is not to be met with conditional obedience.

"If I could know the result of my action, then I would obey," we vow. But would we? Would Abram have set out, as he eventually did, not knowing where he was to go, if he had known that his future included heathen monarchs stealing his wife, famine, war, marauding tribes, dissension in his family, and even the loss of his son? I wonder!

Possibly the step had not been taken because his father had not yet died. "Terah" probably resembled his name, and his strong patriarchal authority and the custom of the day may have demanded Abram's obedient respect.

How easy it is to be sidetracked from the right course of action by a member of one's own family who cannot understand one's aspirations. Omnipotence would one day give an answer to another such disciple, who would excuse himself by saying, "Suffer me first to go and bury my father." The answer would be strong and uncompromising in its apparent harshness, tempered by the experience of the One who spoke, the One who would learn obedience by the things that He suffered. "Let the dead bury the dead," He would say. "And you — you come and follow me!"

Maybe Abram was waiting for a child to be born before he obeyed God. "In thee shall all nations be blessed," Omnipotence had said. Or could the reason for the delay just possibly have been the doing of a beautiful Prime Rib called Contention?

Sarai was instructing Hagar in some homely duty when Abram entered his family abode. "Sarai, I wish to talk with you alone," he said quietly.

"Yes, Abram," she replied simply.

Heavy with emotion, hurting with apprehension, he told her it was time to leave. He watched the shadows rise in her gorgeous eyes, and her hands pressed tightly against her cheeks. She listened in sheer unbelief. He sought desperately to make life in a tent in the wilderness sound like the most exciting thing they had ever done together while his eyes searched her face for her reaction. At the back of his mind an agonizing phrase repeated itself over and over again, "From thy kindred, from thy kindred, from thy kindred!"

Oh, no, Omnipotence. You don't mean Contention! Refusing to admit the thought, Abram battled on: Omnipotence had said to go, and now they must obey. They would be far from home, friends, family, and safety; but Omnipotence, who had commanded, would also be their "shield" and their "exceeding great reward." They would invite

Lot and his wife and family to go, too, and of course Hagar and the servants. The livestock would accompany them — he stopped abruptly. Sarai's exquisite face cut short his monologue, and she said. . . . Well, what did she say? Oh, to know that! But we are not told, and so we cannot know for certain. We only know she went with Abram. But *how* she went or *why* she went we know not. Her character, revealed by many instances in the Scriptures, tells us she loved an argument!

In fact, the name *Sarai* is derived from the same root as Israel and can mean "she that strives" or "a contentious person." So, if her name revealed her character, as it often did in those days, it meant "strife, dispute, and controversy," including the ideas of rivalry and wrangling irritation. I think we can guess, then, how she went. She went obediently, for she called Abram "Lord," but to obey grudgingly or of necessity is not loving obedience that delights the heart of God. You can obey, but as you do, you can make sure the One who commands you understands how much it is costing you! You can lift your cross high enough and wave it in His face long enough to make sure He pays well for nailing you to it! We do not know that Contention acted thus, but we know she had good reason to be upset.

Abram was asking her to leave a life of luxury in an amazingly sophisticated society. She had enjoyed a privileged position among people who had plenty of pleasures to offer her. She had enjoyed security and beauty of countenance that brought admiring court. And now she was being asked to leave all these things — for what? Sand in her food and robbers around her tent? No destination save the vague mirages of her mystic husband's imaginings? No son to propagate their family name, nor hope for one born in desert wanderings? No comfort and companionship of friends and family, save weak Lot's weaker wife?

I wonder if she counseled Abram to simply pray about it instead? To pray and stay, and stay and pray, is easier far than doing God's good will. Or did she want a future revelation of the facts ahead, outlined in clear detail, before she moved?

"No, Contention," I hear godly Abram answer. "We pray *as* we go, not *about* going! The command has come. There is no need for further questions."

How good You are, Omnipotence, to veil the course ahead! We know she went, yet if the veil had been rent and she had seen her husband with her maid and son, the loss of Lot, the kidnap plot, the king's grim and wild harem, would Sarai still have gone? I think not!

"It is too much for thee," Omnipotence declared. "The steps ahead loom far too large for frightened, tiny feet like yours. Just come. I'm out there, and that's all you need to know!"

And so they went, journeying toward the Negev. Contention, still Contention, served her lord. But therein lay the problem. Abram was her lord! Not Omnipotence. Abram was her head, her life, her visible support, her all in all. She loved him and would obey him, and therein lay the danger. She had not learned when to disobey!

Omnipotence shook His head sadly. The time was coming, He observed, when the beautiful little Prime Rib should be the one to counsel Abram to higher acts and deeds than panic, lies, and shame. The testing happened soon. The heathen king observed Contention's beauty. "Lie for me, good wife," her lord commanded. "Tell him you are my sister, or else he will take my life in order to possess you." So lie she did!

When to Disobey Your Husband

There comes a time when Prime Ribs must say no. If God's good laws are contravened by law of man, then no, and no again! Oh, Contention, if God had been your Lord, then Abram would have been the glad recipient of help from you. How much he needed your encouragement to trust in God. How strong you should have been, relaying strength to him. What opportunity to demonstrate dependence! Alas, instead dishonor to Omnipotence! How can a lie be His good will? No way!

Yes, Contention was surely beautiful, but Contention was not nice, Omnipotence observed. She could lie so convincingly and also was adept at other sins! How harsh she was toward her maid. So harsh that with tears poor Hagar fled from her. How did all that come to be? Oh, it was quite simple. Contention was at it again!

Practical by nature, she'd brushed aside her husband's daydreams and taken it upon herself to organize Omnipotence. What He needed at this time, she believed, was her help. A promise had been made that He could not keep. She did not doubt Omnipotence's intentions nor His integrity. She was sure He would have kept His word if He could. But it was obviously not at all a practical promise! The thing to do was act according to the custom of the day and yield to her husband the young and fertile Hagar, that hopefully she might give birth and bear the promised child. And so it was — Ishmael was conceived, and Hagar laughed at Sarai!

"It's all your fault," Contention screamed at Abram, and though that seemed a bit unfair, he yielded Hagar to her thrashing tongue. And so, the poor girl fled from her mistress's face, pregnant and afraid.

Omnipotence, concerned, in loving words recalled her to her duty. He smiled as Hagar in her heathen ignorance obeyed His word, and He sighed as Contention, who should have known better and been sweeter, continued to display her nasty temperament.

One day Omnipotence decided to talk with His earthly friend, now called Abraham. He went to Abraham's tent (imagine that!) to visit, to share the coming judgment of Sodom, to repeat that a baby would be born as heir to Sarai. The tent flap moved as Contention listened furtively to that amazing conversation. Omnipotence frowned as Contention's heart gave forth the raucous laugh of doubt. The heart makes many sounds, produces many notes, but none quite so unpleasant as the laugh of doubt and unbelief.

"Why did Sarah laugh?" Omnipotence asked Abraham.

"I laughed not," she replied with sudden fear.

Contention was her nature. First she argued with her husband, then with Lot's wife, then with Hagar, and now with Omnipotence! She even argued with Him! Not only that, but told a lie as well!

It was time to change her nature and her ways. "But you did laugh," Omnipotence insisted, and suddenly Contention knelt before Him in shame, sick of herself, the lies, the hate, and the pride. "It will be a while, My child, until you laugh again," Omnipotence explained. "But Isaac shall be born, and you will call him 'Laughter.' Then joy shall be your portion. I'll change you, touch your body and your soul and give you a new name — 'Princess' — for so you will be in My sight. Yet I know what it will take before the transformation is accomplished. Because I love you, I will not tell you what is ahead!"

He knew what it would mean — the agonizing birth of Isaac. An old lady in labor, and in the desert, too! No family, friend, or clean home in Haran. Two women in a tent, the rivalry, the boys in fights. The harsh, cruel words that would be used to send her maid and son to certain death. And then the guilt! Oh, what remorse, depression, and loneliness! Poor Contention. If she could know what finally would be, she might not wish to live.

Omnipotence looked onward till He saw old Abraham taking Isaac to his death. The grim, dark morning matched the father's eyes. Omnipotence saw the knife and the wood and heard the panted prayer for strength. He watched His Princess too. Isaac was her son, as well. To be sacrificed! *This* it would take to make a royal lady out of her!

"Contention," He would say, "this is not Abraham's choice alone. Will you withhold your son, your only son, from Me? Will you obey Me, too?" So early in the morning the question was asked. So late in life the answer given. *That's* when the change is wrought — when all we hold most precious is abandoned on the altar of our lives!

The Scripture tells us nothing, yet it must have happened then. No argument is recorded. No screams, no clinging to her son. Just godly meekness in agony yielding life's best gift, producing inner beauty's hushed humility; a princess fit for heaven's home at last!

He changed her, loved her, blessed her, and named her Sarah for the gift she gave. It took ninety years for her to become "God's Princess," a pattern for women everywhere. So take heart, "Contention," if that be your name. He's in no hurry. He has time to spend transforming and transferring His own character to us as we yield to Him.

> *Omnipotence can do it,*
> *Omnipotence will do it,*
> *Because Omnipotence is Omnipotence,*
> *And Omnipotence is power.*

The Stuff in the House

Lot's Wife

The Snake was tired. He'd been putting in a lot of overtime lately, besides which it was extremely hot. The temperature in the Dead Sea area, where he had been slithering around, must have been its usual 120 degrees in the shade. Languidly flicking his tail, he curled himself up for his afternoon nap. Carefully he laid his head on the white "pillar," the strange, gruesome-looking object that reminded him of a woman's body caught in the act of running somewhere, its head twisted awkwardly backward. The Snake affectionately embraced it with his cold-as-death body, for it was a grim monument to a past victory of his.

"You can't see judgment coming when you run that way," he mused. How easy the final victory had been, although he'd nearly lost her at the end. The Enemy had provided her with a marvelous way of escape, which, fortunately, she had resisted.

Years ago in her teen-age days in Ur of the Chaldees the Snake had observed her closely. It was there he became aware that she was a working girl. Not that she ever soiled her pretty hands, but she was a working girl all right. She was working at keeping up with the "Abrams." Green was certainly her color, he had noted. He remembered the great fun he had had at her wedding. He had suggested her wedding dress resembled a tent flap compared to the one provided for beautiful Sarai. As she packed to head for the desert, he decided to officiate at her Stable Sale. He made sure the neighbors who came to buy either insulted or underpaid her. He certainly had her measure. Even he was surprised at the excellent results recorded on her chart, which began to look like a "Dow-Jonah's" depression!

Suddenly a crowd of tourists appeared in the hot desert, and the Snake lay still among the cacti at the foot of the pillar.

"Could this possibly be?" a voice excitedly inquired.

"Is it . . . she?" another asked.

"Well, I don't think so," the preacher replied.

The Snake began to feel sick. The smell of the Enemy was all around, and then suddenly a Bible appeared. The Snake quaked apprehensively as Omnipotence's Book was opened. It was time to go!

"Whether or not Lot's wife looked like this when she was made a pillar of salt, we don't really know," the Reverend began. "However, this weird-shaped object looks enough like her form to recall what our Lord Jesus Christ had to say about her." Beginning at Luke 17:26, he read, "And as it was in the days of Noe [Noah], so shall it be also in the days of the Son of man. They did eat, they drank, they married wives, they were given in marriage, until the day that Noe [Noah] entered into the ark, and the flood came, and destroyed them all. Likewise also as it was in the days of Lot; they did eat, they drank, they bought, they sold, they planted, they builded; but the same day that Lot went out of Sodom it rained fire and brimstone from heaven, and destroyed them all. Even thus shall it be in the day when the Son of man is revealed. In that day, he which shall be upon the housetop, and his stuff in the house, let him not come down to take it away: and he that is in the field, let him likewise not return back. Remember Lot's wife" (17:26-32).

The pilgrims gazed in awe at the grotesque pillar. They would remember!

There are many things Omnipotence has told us to forget. For example, He has forgotten the sins we have confessed to Him. He says, "Your sins and iniquities I will not remember." What Omnipotence has willed to forget, little dust people have no right to will to remember. But there are also things we must remember, that we have no right to forget!

For example, Omnipotence has a Son who knows absolutely all there is to know. Perceiving all that would happen to Him, He still visited this little planet and became a man. He did this so that He might tell us, in language we could clearly understand, the things He wanted us to remember forever. The most important thing we are never to forget is His death. After all, it isn't every day the Son of Omnipotence dies.

"Remember me," He said, breaking the bread and pouring the wine. We must!

"Remember her!" He also said.

"Who?" we ask.

"Lot's wife."

"But she doesn't even have a name!" we say. "Why not remember fair Rachel, Abigail, Esther, Ruth, or Eve?"

"This foolish Rib's story is there for your admonition!" He answers us. "Just as the account of the sin of the children of Israel in the wilderness is written as a warning for your generation, so is the story of Lot's wife."

"Now these things were our examples, to the intent we should not lust after evil things, as they also lusted" (1 Cor. 10:6).

Now we have been learning a little about Omnipotence. We know He is Love, for we know He can cover a woman's sins. We know He can change a lady called Contention, for He is Power. The story of Lot's wife will teach us another facet of Omnipotence's nature, and that is that Omnipotence is Just.

We are to remember Lot's wife because her story teaches us so much about ourselves. Think about the privileges given to her. She was well-acquainted with Abram, a man who had met the "God of Glory" face to face. She had a just and righteous husband. But oh, just watch this Prime Rib. Fastening her eyes upon the cities of the plains, she asked the Snake, whose kingdom those cities comprised, to give them to her. He was delighted to do so!

"Abram can look at the hills if he wants," she decided, "but we will pitch our tent with a view toward Sodom." The fertile plain was filled with all their "stuff," but it was not enough. How tired she was of country life. The cities gleamed from afar and looked like all her heart desired.

Her opportunity came the day the herdsmen fell to fighting. Now was the time to tell lord Abram a thing or two. She and Lot had played second fiddle far too long. The time had come to go their separate ways. She laughed within herself when Abram gave a choice, and close behind her husband's ear encouraged him to choose the selfish best.

The best? Lot's wife sighed in hell. That cruel place sharpens all remembrances!

The Stuff in the House

Omnipotence remembered, too. He has the delightful divine ability to remember forward as well as backward. And so He remembered forward! He thought of all He knew of the twentieth century ahead. The status symbol then would be car, not camel — home, not tent — conforming with group norms in suburbia. The striving, frightened people would be buying far beyond their means, frantic in response to clever, snob advertising influenced by the Snake.

Lot's wife was the first to fall for status symbols of prestige, the house in the "right" neighborhood! She swapped her tent for an address in downtown Sodom! In the "gate area" which was, of course, the most prestigious part. They surely had "arrived," surpassing poor, blind, stupid Abram's dreams of cities built by God!

The house obtained, it was her job to fill it full! "The stuff" was bought and placed and polished, cleaned and worshiped there.

Abram remembered, too. He thought about the frightened messenger relaying news of poor Lot's capture by the kings who came to fight with Sodom. Abram armed his small, but loyal, bodyguard of servants. How well he remembered the pursuit, the fighting, the killing, and the restoring. Lot and all his family "stuff" returned to Sodom's king! Melchizedek, king of Salem, Abram reminisced, had met to bless him, and there revealed to him another facet of Abram's God. Omnipotence, the most high God, he said, was possessor of heaven and earth! And thus when the king of Sodom offered him "the stuff," Abram declined and tartly told him, "Keep it, lest you say, 'I have made Abram rich.' It is God who gives me power to get wealth," he said. "He trusts me with whatever 'stuff' I need to use for Him. I'll hang my weakness on His strength, my poverty on His wealth, and I'll depend on Him!"

43

Abram remembered the look of absurd relief upon the face of Lot's wife. "If you had taken my 'stuff,'" it said. She'd missed the point, Abram reflected. The whole heavenly point! Her goods possessed her, enslaving her to a mindless materialism based on having. Not on needing, not on wanting — just having! When the things you own own you, then you know you are their slave!

Omnipotence's Son looked down the years as well. He knew times would not change. He watched the Snake twisting and tainting the American dream. A twentieth-century sociologist would write a succinct and accurate statement about the situation. "At each income level, Americans want just about twenty-five percent more! The propensity to consume increases more rapidly than our income increases."

So would it be before He came again. Times would not alter much. The hectic hunger for the leisure luxuries of Sodom would increase. The towns made up of tight little circles of people, picking and clawing at each other, would spring up. The club phobia, the sex groups, the deviants popularized, the right wrong, the wrong right. There would be again, as in Lot's time, the rampant homosexuality that would shout to God in heaven to come and see if it could be that bad, and prove that bad to be.

O grace of God to try and warn and make a way. To take the hands of Lot's reluctant family and pull them from judgment! Salvation lay without the city walls. Escape from heaven's fire lay there. Omnipotence groaned aloud as He thought on and years became but moments then, as dark the sky became, and His Son died outside the city, too!

> *How good of God, what grace, what grace,*
> *To take her hand and find a place,*
> *Where she is safe without the wall,*

The Stuff in the House

You'd think she wouldn't mind at all!
The judgment came, the fire fell,
She and her "stuff" were lost in hell!

Remember Lot's wife! The "stuff" was more than heaven's gold to salt-covered Rib. Her mocking sons-in-law more lovely than Omnipotence's Son. Thus, she became a pillar of remembrance.

The Snake returned. The group had gone; the pillar remained, reminding him of those back home! He'd use the "stuff" again — the stuff in the house — his devices would not change. They need not! He laughed. There would be many pillars, each one his own, each one a twisted, conscious monument rooted to the floor of hell forever. The Snake remembered and believed and even trembled, for *he* knew that:

Omnipotence could do it,
Omnipotence would do it,
For Omnipotence is Omnipotence,
And Omnipotence must judge!

Little Dripping Tap
Job's Wife

The Snake had been summoned to see Omnipotence. As usual, he'd been on vice patrol around Job's house, trying to find a way through "the hedge." There was no way! There never is when the hedge is a heavenly barrier. The infuriating thing to the Snake was to see Job and his wife, Little Dripping Tap, living happily and safely inside. Their ten children and their homes lay also within the confines of the hedge.

"It seems to encompass so much," the Snake commented, to no one in particular. "Just look at it! It goes all the way into the valley, protecting his camels, sheep, and oxen; it even circles around the servants who care for them. It's absolutely impenetrable. I know! I've tried!" He had! Watching Job being blessed and blessed again had been a constant challenge and irritation to him. If only he had been allowed to get close enough to Little Dripping Tap's ear, there would have been a good chance of disruption. That was obvious. But when he'd tried to attack, the hedge held him at bay.

Suddenly the summons came. He heard the unmistakable call of Omnipotence and, against every instinct of his spirit, found himself compelled heavenward. On arrival in the throne room, he pretended he'd come of his own free will and accord. After all, it was far too humiliating to admit his compelled attendance! Swaggering among the sons of God, who apparently were nauseatingly thrilled to be there (perish the thought), he tried not to remember his first estate. He couldn't bring himself to look at the empty space over the throne among the other cherubim. He noticed without surprise that his name plaque had been removed; "Lucifer, Son of the Morning" was no more.

The searing love that emanated around him almost induced a scream of sheer torture. To be forever unable to accept, feel, or reciprocate love, when that was all you were originally created for, was an agony only Satan, Father of the Night, could forever know. His vicious hatred spilled out, however, as Omnipotence demanded, "Where have you been and what have you been up to, Snake?" ("As if He didn't know," the Snake ruminated.)

"Vice patrol," he spat out.

"I know," said Omnipotence. "I've watched you stalking around my servant Job. You had to notice him! What a man! Holy in his character, instructing his children in My ways, serving Me faithfully, just like you used to do."

"No wonder! The pay's good!" the Snake retorted. "If You remove the hedge and let me through, let me get near him, then You'll see — he'll become like me. He'll curse You to Your face."

He was just about to give a demonstration when he was reminded somewhat forcefully that cursing was not allowed in heaven. He glanced down toward the object of his accusations, then looked again in unbelief! The sons of God had taken a heavenly "caterpillar" and were demolishing the hedge. Nearly falling out of heaven in his eagerness to destroy his hated enemy, the Snake was recalled by the restraining voice of Omnipotence.

"I will permit you to touch all Job's possessions, but don't lay a finger on him," Omnipotence commanded.

Well, that would do for a start, the Snake decided. He had a momentary qualm that Omnipotence might be up to something, but dismissed the fear in the joy of being permitted to get his hands on Job at last. He pretended that all he had in mind anyway were Job's sheep, oxen, camels, and ten children. How could he ever admit, even to himself, that his evil designs against Omnipotence's worshipers were controlled by His permissive will? He performed an immediate mind-scan on his intended victim. He saw that which had been impossible to see from a distance. Dreadful fears were hovering in Job's heart — fear for his family; fear of losing his home and possessions; fear for his health. The Snake was soon to listen to his victim's anguished cry, "The things I feared have come upon me. I was not fat and lazy, but trouble came!"

Quickly it was done. The Bible says it all happened in a day. It had been a long time since the Snake had been able to work so quickly and easily without any heavenly restraining influence around to hamper him, and he didn't know how much time he had. He kept glancing furtively around to see if the hedge was being replaced. Maybe Omnipotence would change his mind as he watched him touch servants, sheep and oxen, house and children. The smell of death was everywhere, and the Snake really began to feel at home. He was just about to take Little Dripping Tap as well, when he paused. No divine order stayed his hand. He just decided to leave her. Alive and well, she would be much more profitable to his purposes. She would surely be Job's sorest and most poignant trial!

The deed was done. All was gone. Hell waited eagerly for the chorus of Job's blasphemy. The cry of rage must surely come — the angry thunder of a broken man. They heard instead the music of heaven itself. The anthem of worship! "The Lord gave, and the Lord has taken away. Blessed be the name of the Lord."

Screeching in rage, the Snake found himself again in Omnipotence's presence. He longed to ask them to turn the lights down. How they blinded him! However, knowing that holy light was part of heaven's furniture, he hastily made his demands and asked to be excused.

"The last hedge must be removed," he said. "Just let me touch his body. He's far too selfish to care about others; that's why he retains his integrity. Give me his life!"

"No!" said Omnipotence. "His days are numbered and written in My book. You cannot count or know them. You may touch his body, but do not touch his life."

There was no arguing. There never is, for He it is who gives and takes away. But it would be enough to touch Job's body, the Snake decided. The heavenly hedge was gone, and Job lay within his reach. Naked upon the earth, dusty with ashes, streaked with the tears of his mourning, he lay before his God.

"Boils," Snake decided. "I love boils. Nice, juicy, oozy boils. Everywhere! Here, there, and here, and here, and so!"

Procuring a piece of broken pot with which to scrape himself, Job began to hobble on his swollen feet to the refuse heap. The Snake laughed! This was fun. Now surely it would be too much to bear. Now surely Job would learn to hate as he hated, loath as he loathed, curse as he cursed.

Hell waited, as did heaven, yet they heard no curse from the lips of Job. "Yet shall I receive good at the hand of God and shall not receive evil? Though He slay me, yet will I trust in Him!"

Howling like a dog, the Snake tore away to get Little Dripping Tap. "Oh, good," the angels thought with loving sympathy. Now the little Prime Rib would care for Job; she would take him from that dreadful place and tend his wounds. She would cry and say, "Your children and mine. Our tragedy — our pain. For better or worse, for richer, for poorer, in sickness and in health, till death do us part. Come home with me and let my love sustain you."

One angel observed to another, "Two can accomplish twice as much as one. If one falls, the other pulls him up. But if a man falls when he is alone, he's in trouble. On a cold night, two under the same blanket gain warmth from each other. But how can one be warm alone? And one standing alone can be attacked and defeated, but two can stand back to back and conquer."

They waited . . . and waited. . . . Little Dripping Tap had no such ideas. But she had many words. She had never been at a loss for words.

Glaring at Job, she dripped. Drip. Drip. Drip. Drip. Job wanted to scream, but he didn't have the strength. *"Why didn't I turn her tap off years ago?"* he wondered. That had been his problem all along. He hadn't tried hard enough to stop her. It didn't matter that they had seven thousand sheep; "Why didn't the lambs look as healthy this year as last?" she would want to know. It didn't satisfy her to have such a beautiful house, when each of her sons had a better one. It didn't touch her heart when he brought home the fatherless to adopt; it just meant she dripped about all the extra work.

But Job loved her. Oh, how he loved her, and how he

needed her now especially. He didn't want anyone else but his pretty Little Dripping Tap! Beautiful women there were, but none so beautiful as his! He had made a covenant not to look upon any other woman, and she had known it and been secure in his love. But can you believe it? Even that had been the source of more drips. "If only you had other wives, I'd have someone to talk to," she whined.

"No," thought Job, "You can't win when you're married to a dripping tap. When everything's all right, it's bad enough. But when trouble comes, then the faucet opens and the drips become a torrent that cannot be stayed!"

"Curse God and die, old sick man!" she screamed.

"How nice!" thought the Snake. "Encore!"

"You sound like an unbeliever!" Job remonstrated. "It's neither becoming nor helpful to me or you. You know better. The good character of God has been proved to you all your life. His faithfulness and goodness to us have been so wonderfully evident. What we know of Him must now be mixed with faith. I will believe, and you must believe, that the Judge of all the earth does right. You and I must here decide to face affliction in the attitude of worship."

"Your God may be worthy of praise," she retorted, "but not mine! Who can praise a God who lets all this happen to His faithful servant? What thanks is this for all you've done! He laughs at you. He hates you bitterly. Well, I laugh too! You are a fool! He is not worthy of your trust!" And with that she left.

If only Job had acted long ago.
If only he had known "to love" is not to spoil her so.
If only he had cared enough not to allow her attitudes
To drip on everlastingly in empty, pious platitudes.
If only Job had acted long ago,
Then she, with him, could now well face affliction
rare with gratitude!

"If only Prime Ribs would listen to themselves," thought Omnipotence. "Then they might know better than to start dripping when trouble comes. It's a habit. If only they would decide to say, 'I will not drip when there is nothing to drip about.' If they could say to their husbands, 'Husband, please turn off my dripping tap!'

"Suffering doesn't create attitudes; it simply reveals them," said Omnipotence to His Son.

"I know," the Son replied quietly. "Out of the abundance of the heart, the mouth speaketh. It is obvious what Dripping Tap's heart is filled with. Her 'drip philosophy' has led her to the conclusion that God is worth cursing and Job is worth nothing.

"Her line of reasoning goes like this: 'Curse Him, for He has obviously cursed you! So, you obviously must be worth cursing! This is happening to you because you deserve it. You are a sinner, and God is punishing you for it. Look what you have brought upon us all because your sin has offended Him. The innocent don't suffer. Just the wicked. As for wicked hypocrites, they sin most of all! Your sins must surely have been performed in secret places, for I saw none at all!'"

"If I punished their sin with suffering," Omnipotence commented to His Son, "they would each suffer every moment of their days . . . and then it wouldn't be enough! The wages of sin is not suffering; the wages of sin is not boils, or cancer, or the loss of a child, or any other affliction. The wages of sin is death, and without shedding of blood, there is no remission of sins. How could she think suffering could bring atonement?"

His Son replied, "Job's suffering is not as she surmises. It is not an evidence of judgment, but simply an act of Your permissive will, a token, indeed, of Your sure trust in Your servant Job. We trust him with the test, and Our confidence is not misplaced. The fire that tries will surely bring him forth as gold!"

Omnipotence thought two thousand years ahead. Far beyond patriarchal days of sheep and shepherds, He watched a man who lived in twentieth century times. He saw him on his factory bench. He knew the man loved and served Him well. He heard him witness for his Lord and saw him hated by his atheistic co-workers. The man was one Omnipotence had trusted with the care of a mongoloid child! He saw his tortured mind achieve acceptance at the birth and heard his panted prayer for words to speak at work to angry men.

The questions came —

> "Where is your God?
> What God is He?
> How cruel and dark a deity.
> What malice planned against His own,
> To give a child so undergrown,
> So mauled and marred by nature's hand . . .
> What is your God who *this* has planned?"
> The Snake crouched, the world watched,
> And heaven heard the anthem rise,
> As radiant-faced that modern Job
> Received the answer from the skies.

"Can you accept affliction in the attitude of worship?" Omnipotence gently inquired.

The abundant heart answered, "Yes, Lord." And then the words went forth to those unbelieving men, "Oh, how glad I am for her," he said, "how glad I am that Omnipotence gave her to *me* . . . and not to *you!* Praise God!"

Omnipotence rose from His throne in heaven. The elders fell at His feet, casting their crowns before Him.

Job's "friends" had done their worst, and the pressure was almost too great to bear. The time had come to reveal Himself to Job. Not to answer the "whys," but so that Job would need no questions answered . . . ever. The vision of God would be enough. He had heard of Him with his ears, but now his eye would see Him. Only in deep suffering does Omnipotence show Himself so clearly to His children.

"When you can't praise Me for what I allow, Job, praise Me for *who* I am," Omnipotence said. And so he did. How can we help but praise when we see Him as He is? It brings us down to size. When we get a true perspective of ourselves, He's suddenly so obviously larger than our problem. Yes, boils and all! Then we know that our Redeemer liveth! Then we know there'll surely be an end! There has to be. He has promised, "No temptation is too much if I am your anchor." We can trust God to keep the temptation from becoming too strong for us. This He has promised, and He must keep His word. He will show us how to bear temptation's power.

Then the whole trial of suffering with which He trusts us becomes an enlarging experience. Just look at Job. The Bible says he ended up having twice as much of everything . . . that in the latter days he was so blessed and blessed again that the world stood amazed. His Little Dripping Tap must have repented of her attitude, too. Having been revolted at his physical appearance, she would not even touch him. But later we read about ten more children being born to them. Now I know you will agree, Job couldn't achieve "that" without Little Dripping Tap!

Perhaps she finally decided that the God of glory *was* the God of glory. Perhaps she watched that husband of hers forgive and pray for friends who wronged him, relatives who abandoned him, and a wife who failed him. I don't know. But she was reconciled. Their ten children prove it!

Omnipotence walked along the years and tenderly presented Himself to all who suffered as a result of being part of His sin-stricken, fallen creation. One day His Son would die on the cross and defeat death. One day the Snake would be gone forever and with him the source of sin and suffering. Until that day, Omnipotence would allow the suffering to be and would use it as a means of strengthening His children, refining them like precious metals. He would be trusting one here, one there, with His gifts of trials. He would be saying:

I am leading My child to the heavenly land,
I am guiding him day by day.
And I ask him now as I take his hand
To come home by a rugged way.
It's not a way he himself would choose,
For its beauty he cannot see,
But he knows not what his soul would lose
If he trod not that path with Me!

        — Anonymous

  Omnipotence will test you,
  Omnipotence will trust you,
  For Omnipotence is Omnipotence,
  And Omnipotence knows why.

How to Deal With Bitterness
Hannah

Bitterness hurried toward his destination. The Snake had instructed him to arrive before daybreak or his quarry would already have set out on the pilgrimage to Shiloh. He had been told to head for a little house wherein lived a family who was supposed to love Omnipotence. Bitterness privately thought the whole project was foolish. After all, those who were about to make an arduous journey on foot in order to visit the temple and worship Omnipotence would not be likely to give him free room in their hearts.

Sneakily entering the house, he was surprised to discover there was one man living with two Prime Ribs! He chuckled evilly. Now he knew what the Snake had known all along. This was obviously going to be an ideal situation for Bitterness. "One Rib is trouble and trial enough for any man," he said to himself. "This man Elkanah must have had too much sun to take on two at a time!"

He measured himself against the man's heart, but was

rudely rejected by Insensitivity who had been living there for a long, long time and had grown so fat that he filled the place. Next he sidled up to Peninnah's heart, but that was far too small. "Small heart, small mind, too," he muttered, watching her jealously eyeing Hannah, who was obviously the man's favorite. Well, even though it was a small affair, he decided he wouldn't mind moving in. He knew he could enlarge Peninnah's capacity for bitterness. As soon as he opened the door, however, a veritable hoard of occupants — Harshness, Spite, and Hate among them — screamed at him to "get lost, this is our domain!"

He began to wonder if the Snake's computer had blown a fuse. He knew Hannah loved Omnipotence very much. Elkanah's love and favoritism of Hannah was known to be because of her joy in Omnipotence and her resultant desire to please Him and her husband. She was obviously easy to love, Bitterness observed, feeling quite sick. He also noted that Hannah's devotion to the Enemy was an added irritant to Peninnah.

How Hannah had managed to stay so sickly sweet and good in the middle of such an explosive situation, he would never know. Or would he? Maybe the answer was in his notes. He fished in his pocket for his dossier and found the information he required. There it was. She apparently spent many hours talking with heaven. He'd never had a chance to talk to heaven about anything, which made him more bitter than ever, and so he couldn't imagine what there was to go on and on about!

Suddenly his reverie was interrupted. The little caravan was leaving, and he set off behind them. There were many other families making the yearly pilgrimage, and he decided to try his luck elsewhere. He was getting hungry for a good meal of tears and strife! He noted with distaste the children laughing and chattering around their parents' feet. He hated children, but had been around long enough to know they could be used to his advantage.

Suddenly he had an idea. Hastily rereading his instructions, he was reminded that all the little brats belonged to Peninnah, the "unloved" Rib. He watched Peninnah push her little ones away from Hannah's helping hands. The look in both women's eyes caught his attention. Bringing one of Peninnah's children within reach, he tripped up the baby, who sprawled painfully in the dust at Hannah's feet. As he expected, Hannah erupted in a flurry of concern and bent to help the little one. Peninnah let out a shrill scream of rage, telling Hannah to take her hands off her child. Harshness, Spite, and Hate took over the torrent of abuse with great ease and got Peninnah to snipe, "If Omnipotence thought you fit enough to bare children, you would have had some by now. But as you obviously displease Him, you can keep your hands off my offspring. I don't want my children mauled by a God-rejected woman," she ended viciously.

To Bitterness's amazement, Hannah's heart broke. Right there in front of him! It was suddenly wide-open. The gaping wounds were vulnerable and inviting. There was just enough room for him to quickly step inside, which he did, of course. He was never too surprised to take advantage of such an unexpected opening.

Once within, however, he felt very uncomfortable. It certainly wasn't the sort of place he was used to at all. For a start, it was far too clean, and he could sense Hannah's uneasiness at having given room to such a foreign spirit. But by the time they were established at Shiloh, and had arrived at the temple for worship (oh, how Bitterness had shuddered at the mere thought), he had accomplished much. Allowed to remain, he had begun to affect her whole system. Physically she felt very, very sick. Her appetite had gone, and she was weak. This was a great help in any situation, Bitterness smugly reminded himself. Hunger dulled the senses and induced lethargy. Harshness, Spite, and Hate continued to encourage Peninnah to provoke her adversary constantly, which she did, and Insensitivity joined forces to make the whole situation deteriorate.

It was Elkanah's responsibility to give his family a feast after their offering had been accepted by the priest. Omnipotence's law stated clearly that the first-born and his family must have priority where the best portions of food were concerned. Bitterness watched with glee as Insensitivity encouraged Elkanah to offer the worthiest portion to Hannah, right under Peninnah's nose! Elkanah next showed his male chauvinism, by asking his obviously unhappy favorite wife, "Hannah, why are you weeping? Why don't you eat? And why is your heart grieved? Am I not better to you than ten sons?"

Bitterness rolled around inside of Hannah's heart with cackling, unholy mirth. Couldn't the old donkey see he wasn't better than one son, let alone ten? But he stopped laughing abruptly when Hannah refused to answer her husband bitterly. She refused to let Bitterness get in one single word. It was too much. All that marvelous opportunity for Retaliation to join him within her heart, but no, she'd actually barred the doors against him. All she did was weep some more, which began to make him feel very, very uncomfortable. He could be drowned in all this water if he wasn't careful.

Suddenly an awful sensation engulfed him. He realized with horror what it was. Hannah was praying! She was actually talking to Omnipotence. Now Bitterness knew this was extremely dangerous for him. The first lesson the Snake had given him before he had set out on his search-and-destroy mission had been "Never let the victims pray." If they prayed, they would be linked up to high-voltage power, and that could be the beginning of the end of Bitterness! It wasn't the actual prayer that would destroy him, the Snake had explained; it was the available power on the other end of the line that would do that.

Bitterness looked up and around frantically. He had to get reinforcements. Suddenly he noticed a little crack in a heart valve and hastily cabled for Rashness to come to his aid. Immediately he was there, and hastily, as was his character, set to work. Bitterness watched almost admiringly as Rashness actually entangled himself around the prayer promise Hannah was making. He listened unbelievingly as he heard Hannah promise Omnipotence the most stupid and impossible thing in the world. Rashness even got her to vow about it, to give her oath, her promise. He sat listening with evil glee.

"O Lord of hosts," she prayed, "if thou wilt indeed look on the affliction of thine handmaid, and remember me, and not forget thine handmaid, but wilt give unto thine handmaid a man child, then I will give him unto the Lord all the days of his life, and there shall no razor come upon his head" (1 Sam. 1:11). Old Eli the priest had been sitting by a post in the temple watching all this. Suddenly Bitterness stiffened with hatred as he recognized the Snake sitting by the old man's side. "What's he doing here? Checking up on us?" he hissed to Rashness. "Oh, how I hate, hate, hate, hate, hate him!"

"Well, he *is* the expert on accusing the brethren (and the sistren)," Rashness reminded Bitterness. "Just listen to what he's suggesting to old out-of-touch Eli."

It became obvious what the Snake had been suggesting, as Eli rose in pompous majesty, descended on the praying woman who was weeping silently before

Omnipotence, and began a smug prohibition speech. "How long have you been drunk?" he thundered. "Put away the wine!"

Once again Bitterness found himself in the agonizing position of having his hands tied and his mouth shut for him. He struggled defiantly against the strong hands that bound him and recognized that Respect was doing it. Just when had *he* arrived on the scene? Respect smiled and made sure Bitterness could not move at all. He wouldn't even let him move close to Hannah's ear to whisper, "It isn't fair."

Hannah's respect for God's priest was great, even though she was well aware of the old man's weaknesses. She knew he had not dealt with his sinful and backsliding sons, Hophni and Phinehas, who were committing unspeakable acts of debauchery with the women who came to worship at the temple. But God's priest was God's priest as far as Hannah was concerned. She understood how he had made the mistake of thinking she was drunk. She must look a sorry sight indeed by this time, with all this weeping! No, if Hannah was bitter, and bitter she was, she would not allow her bitterness to be joined by Retaliation to attack Elkanah, Peninnah, or Eli. Even Hophni and Phinehas would, she believed, be dealt with by God. He was seated in the judgment seat, so she wasn't going to ask Him to move over and share it with her.

Realizing it was her habit of prayer and her lifelong relationship with Omnipotence that had made her so strong, Bitterness took comfort in the rash promise Hannah had made regarding the promised child.

What if Omnipotence did do the impossible, which is what someone had once dared to say He did all the time. What if the Lord had shut up her womb as Hannah believed? And what if He decided to open it? Bitterness had heard that Omnipotence specialized in doing horrid things like bringing life to dead wombs. He hated that idea with every fiber of his name and nature. Dead wombs were his favorite "hotels" and ideal breeding places for the reproduction of his children — Self-Pity, Shame, and Guilt.

He listened to Eli's promise of a child somewhat skeptically, but with a sort of sinking feeling. Suddenly his world was flooded with light, and to his horror, Hannah appeared in front of him. Opening her heart, she glared at him, and in the most loud and ferocious way commanded him in the name of Omnipotence to leave.

"Get out! There's no room for two of you!" she ordered.

"Two of us?" Bitterness asked, wondering who she could mean, as Rashness had departed as soon as his work was done.

"Yes," Hannah answered, "two of you. Belief is coming to stay!"

With that, Bitterness found himself picked up in Belief's strong hands and hurled on his neck in the temple area. He scurried quickly away, needing to find a home as soon as possible. He couldn't possibly return to the Snake with a truthful report of dismissal on the job!

How bitter he felt about Hannah. How he hated her. What ever could he do to hurt her? He nervously twisted his body in knots as he ran, searching frantically for another resting place. Suddenly he saw Recant hurrying toward him. Hastily Bitterness pointed in Hannah's direction, gave Recant quick instructions, and disappeared into the night howling with hunger and remorse.

Recant arrived breathless at the little house and realized he need not have hurried. It would be four years before the child was weaned and his opportunity approached. There was even time before the precious baby arrived, so he could begin to do some of his work early. Rashness had done a good job, he observed, and now it was his turn.

The promised baby was born, and he watched Hannah tend him. "How ever could she give little Samuel away?" he asked himself.

"All these years you've waited," he intoned into her ear. "Look how special and beautiful he is. He's a miracle baby. God obviously intended for you to look after him. Why should someone else have all that worry when it's your responsibility? And what about all that money Elkanah has spent on you and the baby?" he continued. Hannah thought about that. Peninnah had not been willing to share any of her things, that was for sure. Selfishness, who had always been around Peninnah's heart, had seen to that. Elkanah had had to go out and buy everything new.

"And so, what's that husband of yours going to say when his favorite son disappears?" Recant inquired. "And what about your adversary? How she will enjoy watching you pack up your baby things and fold away the little clothes. I'll see to it that she constantly reminds you that you gave your child into the unscrupulous care of Hophni and Phinehas, who will be sure to teach him how to lie with the women at the Temple gate!" And so it went on . . . and on . . . and on.

Four years later Recant had to grudgingly admit defeat. Belief and Respect, great enemies of Bitterness, had been joined by the greatest of all — Determination. It was he who enabled Hannah to prepare a sacrifice and help her little Samuel walk the long way to Shiloh, away from her care forever. Rashness, seeing the unbelievable happen, headed for the desert for a thousand-year vacation. He

trusted the Snake would be too busy to find him. Recant
stood with the parents in front of Eli, desperately seeking a
last opportunity. But he was totally ignored as Hannah and
Elkanah stood before Eli with the child Samuel in their
arms. Omnipotence smiled and the angels laughed as
Hannah said, "Oh my lord, as thy soul liveth, my lord, I am
the woman that stood by thee here, praying unto the Lord.
For this child I prayed; and the Lord hath given me my
petition which I asked of him: therefore also I have lent
him to the Lord; as long as he liveth he shall be lent to the
Lord" (1 Sam. 1:26-28).

Omnipotence dispatched his special guardian spirit
to care for little Samuel. He was going to need extra protection while he was among such awful corruption, and in the
temple at that. He would be all right though. Hannah's
prayers would ascend constantly before Him, to be lovingly answered by a God who would not allow such sacrifice to go unrewarded. Samuel would become judge,
priest, and prophet to all Israel, known throughout the
land, reverenced and loved by all.

Heaven watched as little Samuel knelt to pray as his
mother had taught him. Four years had been enough —
enough to teach him all he needed to know.

"You've been lent to Omnipotence," Hannah had explained. "He would like to borrow your life, and your
father and I have given Him permission to do so for as long
as you live. But you must remember always how much I
love you and will pray for you. When we both live with
Omnipotence in heaven, we will be together again.

"Eli will show you how to worship Omnipotence
and learn His will and Word. Little Samuel, I have
given Omnipotence permission to use you, but there
must come a time when you must give Him permission as
well. When that time comes, you will be on your own.

Heaven will wait for your answer. Good-by, my little son, whom I love so much. I commit you to Him!"

Meanwhile, back in the dungeon, Bitterness inquired of Harshness whether there was any hope for him to enter Hannah's heart when she returned alone from her great sacrifice in the temple. He wanted to know what her reaction had been when Peninnah and all her children reminded her searingly of her great loss.

Harshness sadly replied that instead of repenting of her foolishness, Hannah had sung a horrid song of praise to Omnipotence. They both shuddered. They knew what that meant. Oh, how Praise tormented them above all others! Far away, they heard Hannah's song:

My heart rejoiceth in the Lord, mine horn is exalted in the Lord: my mouth is enlarged over mine enemies; because I rejoice in thy salvation.

There is none holy as the Lord: for there is none beside thee: neither is there any rock like our God. . . .

He will keep the feet of his saints, and the wicked shall be silent in darkness; for by strength shall no man prevail.

The adversaries of the Lord shall be broken to pieces; out of heaven shall he thunder upon them: the Lord shall judge the ends of the earth; and he shall give strength unto his king, and exalt the horn of his anointed (1Sam. 2:1, 2, 9, 10).

Bitterness and his fellows howled with rage and pain as the name of Omnipotence's Son fell from Hannah's lips. Would the Enemy's victories never cease? Apparently not. Three more sons and two daughters followed little Samuel to bless Hannah's life.

"Praise to Omnipotence," sang the angels, and they flung their words around the heavens, words that seemed to say:

Omnipotence could do it,
Omnipotence would do it,
For Omnipotence is Omnipotence,
And Omnipotence is life.

How to Deal With a
Difficult Man

Abigail

The Snake had tried everything he knew, but nothing had worked. This wretched Prime Rib was apparently untemptable. "Contemptible, too," he muttered. He had been sure marriage to Nabal would do it. After all, Nabal meant "fool," and so he was, the Snake thought proudly! "How then," he asked himself, most vexed with the whole thing, "could a Prime Rib married to a fool be so horribly and consistently good?"

Something had to be done. The thing to do was simply get rid of her. Now murder was something very near the Snake's heart. He was the father of such and had a book containing all the methods and variations that could be used. It was one of the most popular books in hell and was never in the library when he wanted it. Turning to the chapter on "Reasons for Murder," he thumbed through the pages. "Anger" seemed the easiest way to go, but who could get angry enough at Abigail to kill her?

"Maybe you'll have to get someone so angry at Nabal that he'll kill them both!" Lust suggested.

The Snake appeared in David's fugitive camp to see if there was any way he could exploit the potentially dangerous situation he had been informed about.

It was sheep-shearing time, and parties were always given by the owner of the sheep for his shearers. They were great opportunities to exploit because of all the wine imbibed by the participants, and the Snake came upon Self-Indulgence and Drunkenness hovering hopefully on the scene.

Now David and his band of followers had been hiding out in the mountain strongholds, hunted by Saul and his soldiers. They were enjoying a respite at the moment and had been free to get on friendly terms with the shepherds who cared for Nabal's animals.

Nabal's cattle and sheep were grazing far from home and were vulnerable to attacks by thieves. It was dangerous work being a shepherd in those days, and the men had been overwhelmingly grateful for the protection David had graciously and freely provided.

Now the time for celebration had come. The sheep were to be sheared; the party was planned. David and his men sent a message saying they would be glad to join in the fun.

The Snake saw his chance. Tempting Nabal to respond in his typically rough and rude manner, he achieved the desired result. "And Nabal answered David's servants, and said, 'Who is David? and who is the son of Jesse? there be many servants now a days that break away every man from his master'" (1 Sam. 25:10).

It was just the sort of situation the Snake had dreamt about. Now David was angry. *Really angry!* Knowing that anger is the root from which the fruit of murder can result, the Snake rejoiced. Gathering four hundred of his men and commanding them to gird on their swords, David set off to wreak vengeance on Nabal, his family, servants, sheepshearers — everyone! It was enough to make the Snake nearly split his skin. How many innocent people would die, and among them beautiful Abigail!

Hearing what was happening, one of the servants of Nabal, fearing for his life, came to his mistress and poured out his fears. "Behold, David sent messengers out of the wilderness to salute our master; and he railed on them. But the men were very good unto us, and we were not hurt, neither missed we any thing, as long as we were conversant with them, when we were in the fields: They were a wall unto us both by night and day, all the while we were with them keeping the sheep. Now therefore know and consider what thou wilt do; for evil is determined against our master, and against all his household: for he is such a son of Belial, that a man cannot speak to him" (1 Sam. 25:14-17).

Abigail stood quite still. She felt very small and frightened and desperately inadequate. Her life seemed to pass quickly in front of her eyes, and she saw herself as a young girl being given in marriage to the arrogant, wealthy Nabal, son of the rich man of the village. She had had such dreams about their life together. Her husband was of the house of Caleb and knew well what it was to serve Omnipotence and live a godlike life before Him.

But it had not been many weeks before she had seen that he cared not for Omnipotence, His words or His ways. Perhaps he had had too much too soon, or perhaps the authority he had inherited went to his head. But regardless of what had caused it, for years now Nabal's reputation had been that of a "fool — a son of Belial, a churlish and evil man." He had become almost impossible to work for, refusing to discuss his business affairs with the very men whom he expected to run them for him. And worse, he had become evil in all his doings. Add to all that his dreadful drinking habits, and you get the picture. He never got drunk. He got *very* drunk!

Abigail sighed. Abigail knew it was so. Abigail had lived with an exceptionally difficult man for an incredible number of hard years.

She thought of going to Nabal and pleading with him to *do* something. Then she remembered the last time she had remonstrated with him over some harsh treatment of her maidens and how he had turned and railed on her, even as he had railed on David's servants. He had a foul mouth, and she couldn't stand to hear Omnipotence's name taken in vain like that again. Coming from a good family herself and being a beautiful, intelligent, and wise woman, she had been taught to conduct herself in a proper fashion, and Nabal's churlish attitude was a constant source of embarrassment to her.

What should she do? Should she simply cast herself upon Omnipotence's mercy and pray for His intervention on their behalf? She thought of all she knew about Omnipotence. She believed He was alive and could see the situation. She knew her Lord both avenged and withheld His judgments upon the children of men. She trembled at this, knowing Nabal deserved all Omnipotence could send! But she believed that Omnipotence set up whom He willed and that He loved *holy* and good men. And if He loved holy men, was it not reasonable to suppose He loved holy women, too? She believed Omnipotence was good and just. Therefore, in her mind she committed herself to all she knew of Him and decided to try and *do* something about the desperate situation. She dared to believe

Omnipotence loved her and would go with her and protect her.

Abigail was committed to Omnipotence. She was also committed to her marriage. She knew marriage was Omnipotence's idea, and all His ideas were "very good." Just because one partner had not done his part didn't mean the marriage idea was bad. She had said her vows and intended to live and die by them — "for better or for worse," she had vowed. Yes, Abigail was committed to Nabal — and to her marriage!

The Snake hated her line of reasoning. He tried to get her to see how incompatible she and Nabal were. This surely was excuse enough to abandon him and save her own skin. "Incompatibility is sure grounds for divorce," he intoned, trying to sound sympathetic. He would like to see Nabal suffer the indignity of his wife's exodus before he was slaughtered, and he knew Abigail could not get very far from David's fleet men. To his amazement, he was brought back from his reverie by Abigail's firm voice telling him that incompatibility was the reason for *marriage,* not the reason for *divorce!*

"Who's compatible, anyway?" she demanded. "That's why Omnipotence put us in families in the first place. He knows as we learn to give and take, adjust and adapt, we fill up that which is lacking in the other, and two incompatible people slowly become one compatible couple to Omnipotence's great glory."

"Well, you didn't change Nabal much," sneered the Snake.

"I don't think I did," admitted Abigail. "But you see, I changed me, hoping that would produce a change in him. And anyway, I'm not through yet! I intend to continue to try, because you see, you old Snake, I am committed to Omnipotence, and He is committed to my marriage, and so I am committed to Nabal, fool though he be."

And with that she saddled her donkey, took some presents with her, and set off at a cracking pace to meet her would-be murderer!

The Snake was amazed. He had not realized how realistic Abigail was. To be realistic about marriage — not idealistic — was not at all helpful to his divorce ratings. Setting off after her into the wilderness, he knew it was useless to tempt her to be unfaithful to her mate. When you are committed to your Maker, your marriage, and your mate, not even a gorgeous hunk of angry man like David is going to change your mind. The Snake did suggest to her that she forget the material gifts she had brought and offer herself instead. After all, she was absolutely gorgeous, and all that riding in the sun and wind had simply enhanced her beauty. The chemistry would obviously be just right between her and David, and this could be a way to save her own skin.

"Why risk your life for Nabal when you could entice David? Why not cheat? Omnipotence would understand. It hasn't been much fun being married to Nabal, but just think of the exciting times you could have with David!" concluded the Snake.

Abigail slipped from her donkey and fell at David's feet. Her heart was pounding and her voice shook. Ignoring the Snake's suggestions, she set about saving her husband's life.

"Now, how absolutely beautiful," Omnipotence observed in heaven. "Just see how My child shows no desire for Retaliation. What a wonderful opportunity she has at this moment. For all the times Nabal has come drunk to her bed, for all the times he has beaten and mistreated her, for all his evil ways, bad words, and arrogant deeds, now she could really get her own back and let him have it. David is

showing obvious sympathy. Look! She gains his ear with
her tactful words. Now she could send him merrily onward to finish off her husband, for she sees she is safe. But
no! She is committed — "till death do us part." And how I
love her for it! Now I shall be her help. If only all my other
little Prime Ribs down the ages, who are learning to live
with difficult men, would be as she and say, 'What can I do
for him?' instead of 'How can I get rid of him?' Then I
would rejoice."

The angels watched in fascination as Abigail began to
deal with the angry man before her. She had lived with
Anger for so long that she had practiced well those an-
tidotes that work for such times of confrontation. She
knew she must agree where she could with the reasons for
his anger. She must tell him she saw his point of view.
Nabal *was* a worthless fellow, she agreed. David was right
to be angry about his churlish behavior. She next admitted
her wrong in the matter. This was more difficult. (It always
is!) However, she sought some way of taking the wrong
upon herself, some way to find something she could be
sorry about, so she could ask for his forgiveness. She found
a way in the end, confessing that she had been too preoc-
cupied to visit with David's messengers when they came,
or she would certainly have complied with their request.
For this she sought his mercy.

How tempting it was for her to cry out, "It isn't fair. I
couldn't help it! I don't deserve this." But this is not the
way to deal with an angry man! "A soft answer turns away
wrath," Omnipotence's book declares. And so it does. And
did!

Seeing David respond so favorably to her immediate
overtures, Abigail dared to offer some advice. She reminded him of Omnipotence's love for him — His plan for
his life as king of Israel. "Oh, David, my lord, you don't

need to avenge yourself, or even protect yourself," she concluded, "for you are locked up inside Omnipotence's purse!"

David's anger disappeared. Abigail's beauty, wisdom, counsel, and concern, and above all her great courage, won his heart. He was tempted to pick her up and carry her away to his mountain cave, but her purity and obvious commitment to Nabal stayed his hand . . . and his desires. What a woman! The man Nabal was even more of a fool than he knew him to be. To have such a wife and treat her so! He hastily turned his men back before he began to get angry all over again. Blessing Abigail for her words of wisdom and restraint, he sent her on her way.

Arriving home, Abigail found her husband far too drunk to even talk to, and so she held her peace. In the morning she would try again. She would tell him how God had delivered them from death and given them another chance to work out their problems. She would describe her part in saving his life at the risk of her own. Then surely he would respond to her with love. Yes, she would try, and go on trying and trying again.

The morning dawned, and Abigail told him all. Nabal's heart died in him, and he followed suit several days later. Abigail nursed him lovingly until the end. She had done everything she could, and so there was no guilt. Omnipotence had intervened. She was set free.

The moral of the story is not: do the right thing, and Omnipotence will give you a man like King David as a reward! The moral of the story *is:* learn by Omnipotence's help how to live with a difficult man and how to cope with an angry man. This way Omnipotence can use your testimony to help all the other people who are doing the same!

> *Omnipotence can do it,*
> *Omnipotence will do it,*
> *For Omnipotence is committed to your marriage,*
> *And Omnipotence is help!*

How to Commit Adultery When Your Husband's Out of Town

Bathsheba

The Snake was busy editing Lust's manuscript. The spelling was dreadful, but the ideas were as bad as they could be, and the Snake knew it would be a hot-selling item on the market. In fact, he knew exactly who the first purchaser would be. Beautiful Bathsheba. She'd buy it! He flicked his tail in evil delight.

Putting the finishing touches to the "porno" cover, he deliberated over the title. With a flash of evil genius, he came up with a best-seller title: *How to Commit Adultery When Your Husband's Out of Town*. "How about that?" he asked Lust, who drooled approvingly and rushed away to present it to Uriah's wife.

She was going to be harder to entice than Little Dripping Tap, he observed. Her strength of character and courageous, fiery temperament indicated a positive response to crushing adversity. Her husband, fighting Israel's battle far away, would be an easy target, but something told him that was not the way to go. Sometimes it was easier to fall for Temptation in ordinary, everyday situations — like . . . well, like the very one he found Bathsheba in as he arrived at her front door. Her husband was out of town! That was all. But that was enough.

Omnipotence allowed Temptation to knock at the door. Bathsheba opened it and smiled. "Come in," she said. Now Temptation is not sin. If it were, then Jesus was a sinner, because Jesus was tempted. In fact, we read in Omnipotence's book that the Holy Spirit actually led Jesus into the wilderness to meet Temptation. He knew who stood behind Temptation's shadow (that is, the Snake), and He knew the experience of resisting would result in His returning in the fullness of the power of God. No, Temptation is not sin, but to obey his evil suggestions is!

Bathsheba was not a bit afraid of him. After all, he was very familiar. In fact, he was "common to man." Everyone she knew was acquainted with him, so why be suspicious? She had faced him before and had usually been able to ignore his suggestions.

But this time it was different. She was lonely. Uriah had been away such a long time. She was bored. There was nothing to do. She was also depressed. She was not usually so, but then Temptation is not stupid enough to approach us when we are at our best! No, it's when we are vulnerable, hurting in some area of our life, that he cunningly appears with his directives. And so it was with Bathsheba.

The beautiful Prime Rib noticed her visitor was carrying a new book in his hand. She didn't know it had been written especially with her in mind. She was also unaware that it was straight from the pit of hell! There appeared to be an intriguing picture of her king on the front which captured her attention. At least it seemed to be intriguing until she noticed he was naked! She gasped in horror and her eyes traveled to the title, *How to Commit Adultery When Your Husband's Out of Town.* She looked long and hard into Temptation's eyes. They had a hypnotic quality about them. They appeared to be calm and reassuring as if to say, "Don't run away! Just give me a chance to explain the whole idea. Just take it in your hand and think about it. You've plenty of time on your hands . . . what you need is a good book to go to bed with!"

Did she *really* think he wanted her to go to bed with a *book,* chortled the Snake?

Having given Bathsheba their ideas, Temptation and Lust walked quickly across the narrow streets of Jerusalem to David's palace.

"Sweet psalmist of Israel," they began, "anointed one of God, man after Omnipotence's heart, we're so glad to find you at home!"

They could have made a serious mistake at this point, for their words brought a stab of guilt to David's heart. This was the time "kings went forth to war," and the sweet psalmist of Israel should *not* have been at home at all. Laziness was sitting comfortably in David's throne room, and he it was who opened wide the door for Temptation. Self-indulgence was busy making the king's bed, for it was "late in the day," and the monarch had just arisen.

Temptation began to get excited. He wasn't the least bit awed by the king's person, for he was used to being around important people. Temptation "happens" to the best and the worst of us, you know. No, he was excited because he knew this was going to be his lucky day.

They escorted the king out to the flat roof of the palace to enjoy the evening air and maneuvered him into a good position in line with Bathsheba's house.

Meanwhile, back at the villa, Uriah's lovely and lonely wife had begun to read that book. Arriving at the chapter entitled "How to Tell Him You're Available," she chose the casement window approach. It seemed simple. Just a matter of "how much" she would display to the king's gaze! It was quite a lot, observed Temptation admiringly.

The king looked! Of course the first look isn't sin. He couldn't help seeing the lovely girl carefully posed in the casement picture frame. But the second look? And the third and the fourth — that surely *was* iniquity. And David knew it. And David did it!

There is a verse in Omnipotence's book that says, "An evil man conceives an evil plot, labors with its dark details, and brings to birth a child — treachery and lies!"

But David was not evil, you say! And some say it was Bathsheba who gave us her philosophy of life in Proverbs 31. Remember? "A good wife, who can find? She is far more precious than jewels. The heart of her husband trusts in her, and he will have no lack of gain" (31:10,11 RSV). Here were two human beings who were fantastic people, lovers of God and His Word. True. But the heart of man is deceitful above all things and desperately wicked! Out of that heart come evil thoughts, adultery, murder, theft, covetousness, wickedness, deceit, blasphemy, pride, and foolishness.

To know yourself is to be fully aware of all that. To know yourself is to believe you are capable of all that inherent sinful nature of yours longs to do. To know yourself is to watch yourself, lest you enter into temptation. To say ever so proudly, "I would not, I could not *ever* commit adultery," is to issue a challenge to hell to which you are not equal! You are the very person who "thinking that she stands, will surely fall." You cannot know the set of circumstances in which you may find yourself at your most vulnerable point — circumstances that will find you smiling at Temptation and accepting his invitation. Yes, you! I'm talking to you. Are you stronger than David, king of Israel? More powerful than Uriah's gracious wife? Oh, little modern Bathsheba, listen to the warnings of Scripture and know yourself!

To know yourself is to understand your God-given human sexuality. Omnipotence likes sex. He thought of it first. He made it a wonderfully creative, constructive, strong drive in the make-up of our human personality. We must know ourselves as sexual beings and love ourselves as God Himself loves us. But how we need to watch. For the Snake will surely seek to use and pervert all God's good gifts to man.

To know yourself is to grow in humility, and to grow in humility is to grow in dependence on Omnipotence, and to grow in dependence is to lock and bar the door against Temptation. To know yourself in this right way is to watch yourself with prayer at all times, and then the ability to stop yourself becomes a reality.

The problem was to stop! Having been caught completely off guard in a state of loneliness and boredom, unsatisfied sexual desires at a premium, she who had previously tossed her head and said so proudly, "I could not, I would not," did!

The Snake laughed. "You will and you shall, little Bathsheba," he said. "Always! If you are hopefully looking out your window showing what you shouldn't, I'll provide a looker and a taker. Just give me time!"

"An evil man conceives an evil plot, labors with its dark details and brings to birth a child — treachery and lies." David had looked twice! There's an old Chinese proverb that says, "You can't stop the birds from flying over your head, but you can stop them from nesting in your hair!" David didn't, and the eggs were hatching!

The plot was conceived and he was now into the second stage. He began to labor with its dark details. He sent a messenger to find out who she was. He discovered she belonged to one of his most devoted servants and friends. Uriah had fought side by side against Saul's men, had shared the fear and terrors of exile, and had proved his devotion to his king and country. Listed as one of David's mighty men in the Book of 2 Samuel, he stands tall and straight, a man among men.

Yet, David labored on! He sent a message to Bathsheba, knowing full well whose she was, and called her to him. She accepted . . . she came . . . willingly.

The problem was that the whole affair looked so exciting. How flattering to have the king's attention. What a catch! Excitedly she dressed herself, pretending all was under control. Arguing with her conscience, she reasoned thus, "Well, what's wrong with it anyway?" It had been a long time since she had enjoyed male company. They would have an interesting and stimulating evening together. Why, they could talk about the war.

"Who's kidding who?" the Snake asked, listening in to her busy and excited thoughts.

Things were going wonderfully well, he decided. He listened to her praying a familiar prayer, one which many Prime Ribs prayed when they were enjoying the pleasures of sin too much to stop. She was saying, "Lord, make me holy, but not just yet. Lord, I really want to be the best for You, but not just now. This is too much *fun!*"

The silly little fool was not even going to accept Omnipotence's "way of escape," the Snake observed. He sneered at the Almighty and inquired if He was about to tear the two apart by sending a few angels down.

Omnipotence quietly and sadly replied, "That is not My way. My ways of escape are not such massive displays of dynamite; they are ordinary and available things."

"Like what?" the Snake spat.

"Like eyelids and feet," said Omnipotence.

"Eyelids and feet?" Even the Snake was surprised.

"I provided some very simple and available ways to escape their temptation," replied Omnipotence. "Eyelids and feet for David, clothes for Bathsheba, and a tongue that can say 'no' as well as 'yes.' They chose to ignore them!"

With Bathsheba pregnant, David labored further, bringing forth treachery and lies. Uriah must come home and sleep with his wife.

Summoned from the battlefield on some pretense or other, the honorable man refused to so enjoy himself while his fellow soldiers died for Israel's sake. So David got him drunk! Then surely he'd go home to wife and bed! But Uriah proved himself a mighty man indeed. A better man drunk than David was sober, he still refused. "So, he must die!" the king decreed.

Carrying in his hand his own death warrant (though he knew it not), the faithful soldier traveled back to Joab, his commander, who placed him against impossible odds and treacherously left him to die, exactly as David had instructed. *Murder now . . . what next?*

Treachery and lies! Lies upon lies there must be. I mean, how do you tell Bathsheba you've just murdered her husband? How do you justify so vile an act to faithful Joab? What words to make wrong look right to servants who watched David's sin? The hardened heart adds sin to sin to sin. The more people who know, the more you need to "labor with the dark details" of your plot. The more people who must be silenced, the more intrigue is necessary . . . until through some means God faces you and says, "Stop!

91

It is enough! *You* are the man who deserves to die for this, not Uriah or the baby boy sin bore. *You* are the man who stole your best friend's wife and stole his life as well. *You are the man I am displeased with.*"

How long it took for David to repent, we do not know. But this we know . . . the instant he repented, God *forgave!*

"I have sinned!" he cried.

"And I have forgiven you," replied Omnipotence at once.

How easy. If that is all there is to being forgiven, let's sin more, you say? God forbid! Forgiven you may be, but, oh, the bodies all around that cannot be brought back to life! The dark results of sin are there, like Joab's shattered trust and Bathsheba's broken heart. To lose her child and husband was quite a price to pay for a few sweet stolen moments.

Forgiven you may be, but the future is yet to come. See Absalom, David's favorite child, his father's grim example held before him, deal treacherously with his own and end up raping his father's wives in sight of all Israel. What could the king say to that? Nothing. His mouth was shut. Yes, forgiven you may be, but is it worth the mess? The price you pay, the pain you bring to others? Never.

Your husband is out of town? You fell? Your husband is not out of town! You fell? Repent! You will? You are forgiven then. You do not know what to say? Use David's words; I know none better:

> Have mercy on me, O God,
>   according to thy steadfast love;
>   according to thy abundant mercy
>   blot out my transgressions.
> Wash me thoroughly from my iniquity,
>   and cleanse me from my sin!

When Your Husband's Out of Town

For I know my transgressions,
  and my sin is ever before me.
Against thee, thee only, have I sinned,
  and done that which is evil in thy sight,
so that thou art justified in thy sentence
  and blameless in thy judgment.
Behold, I was brought forth in iniquity,
  and in sin did my mother conceive me.

Behold, thou desirest truth in the inward being;
  therefore teach me wisdom in my secret heart.
Purge me with hyssop, and I shall be clean;
  wash me, and I shall be whiter than snow.
Fill me with joy and gladness;
  let the bones which thou hast broken rejoice.
Hide thy face from my sins,
  and blot out all my iniquities.

Create in me a clean heart, O God,
  and put a new and right spirit within me.
Cast me not away from thy presence,
  and take not thy holy Spirit from me.
Restore to me the joy of thy salvation,
  and uphold me with a willing spirit.

Then I will teach transgressors thy ways,
  and sinners will return to thee.
Deliver me from bloodguiltiness, O God,
  thou God of my salvation,
  and my tongue will sing aloud of thy deliverance.

O Lord, open thou my lips,
  and my mouth shall show forth thy praise.
For thou hast no delight in sacrifice;
  were I to give a burnt offering,
  thou wouldst not be pleased.
The sacrifice acceptable to God is a broken spirit;
  a broken and contrite heart, O God,
  thou wilt not despise.

(Psalm 51, RSV)

You prayed it? Good!

How good and great of God to deal with our transgression and our darkest sin. What grace. What mercy. Forgiven and restored, the two who lost their child received

another! And another — named Nathan, and through his
line came the Christ who would make David's name abide
forever.

Omnipotence could do it,
Omnipotence would do it,
For Omnipotence is Omnipotence,
And Omnipotence is grace.

In-Laws and Out-Laws
Ruth

My God Is King married Pleasure one day. "That's an explosive situation if ever there was one," the Snake observed. Old Elimelech and Naomi had names befitting their characters! As the evil one looked ahead in time (although it was not given to him to be omniscient, that being the prerogative of Omnipotence), he saw enough to know there was a famine ahead. A famine that would mean hard times for Bethlehem. Bethlehem means "City of Bread," but soon there would be none and the cupboards would be bare. The Snake decided he could use the situation to incite Pleasure to insist on "the best" and nag Elimelech into moving to Moab.

Coming from a well-to-do family, Pleasure was not attuned to adversity. Her life had been pleasantly full of good things, and when trouble loomed large on her horizon, she had but one desire . . . self-preservation! She could see no point whatsoever in staying with the sinking ship.

"Let's go where the food is," she said to Elimelech. "That's the obvious thing to do."

Now Elimelech did not have access to Matthew 4:4, where Jesus says that man does not live by bread alone, but by every word that proceeds out of the mouth of God, but he *did* know that God had not promised to bless Moab. In fact, the whole history of Moab and its inhabitants was a grim lesson to God's people about seeking the easy and pleasure-filled way of life. The folk who lived in that region had descended from Lot's eldest daughter through the child conceived by her own father in a mountain cave. "Well, that was a good start!" sniggered the Snake. The whole tone of life in Moab was of a "Sodom" life style. Though the people had some knowledge of Jehovah and His ways, idol worship abounded, so the Snake decided it would be a great place for anyone to live!

Elimelech knew all these things. He also had access to heavenly information that told him the little city of Bethlehem had been bathed in the promises concerning Omnipotence's purposes and designs. To abandon Bethlehem was to move out of range of the blessings and promises of God.

"It's easy to believe the promises when your stomach's full," whined Pleasure, "but I'd rather trust my own judgment when we've a family to feed." *A full stomach now feels better than an empty stomach and mere words,* she thought privately.

Elimelech looked at their children, Mahlon and Chilion. Instantly the Snake saw his chance.

"No wonder you named them so," he began. "Sickness and Pining they are and have been since the day they were born. To expose them to a severe famine could not be your heavenly Father's wish."

So, My God Is King changed his name to My Wife Is Queen and they set off for Moab.

It was not easy to leave Bethlehem. It never is. To leave the place of blessing and go with Pleasure, to have her rule your life instead of Omnipotence, can only result in disaster. In time, it did.

True, there was bread in Moab, but it was not the bread of heaven. Soon Elimelech, Mahlon, and Chilion died, and Pleasure was left. But how much Pleasure can be left when Pleasure is all alone? Pleasure requires company and comfort to survive, and when none is available, the transient happiness departs leaving one's heart desolate.

She was not, however, completely alone. Ruth and Orpah remained. God *is* Blessing. He cannot help Himself. He has to be so positively good toward us, even when we are so positively bad toward Him. Because that's what He's like! He had brought two beautiful girls into Naomi's life. Daughters of Moab, true, but they became daughters in the true sense to Naomi. In fact, Naomi was hard put to think of any girls in Bethlehem whom she would rather have seen married to her beloved boys. And now they proved their worth. Sitting around the little table in that small house in Moab, the discussion continued well into the night.

"What shall we do?" They couldn't stay in Moab. Not three women alone. It was not safe! They could ask the girls' fathers to receive them back into their childhood homes and thereby hope to remarry. Naomi, of course, would be unacceptable, but at least that would take care of the girls.

Suddenly Naomi looked up. "I'm going home," she announced quietly. A great peace enveloped her. "City of my God, Bethlehem, I'm coming home," she said almost to herself. Omnipotence heard her and was glad.

Ruth and Orpah watched their mother-in-law's face. They loved her. Why or how we know not, but love and loyalty, respect and trust were there.

"We'll come, too," they said simply.

Naomi looked helplessly at each. She knew she should remonstrate and say no. But they were all she had. She loved them. They were the only links left with the three men who had meant all the world to her. Pleasure, who had gone out *full*, was about to return empty and in Bitterness.

"Call me not Naomi," she was soon to say. "Call me Mara: for the Almighty hath dealt very bitterly with me. I went out full, and the Lord hath brought me home again empty" (Ruth 1:20,21).

No, Naomi! Was it Omnipotence who led you to Moab? Don't blame Him!

The three women set out on the long, dangerous journey. Bitter though she was, Naomi began to suffer pangs of remorse, and she finally stopped and faced her daughters-in-law.

"You must return," she said. "How can I be so selfish. To take you home with me simply resigns you to perpetual widowhood. No Israelite will marry a heathen girl lest he mar his inheritance. Your chances for security and a happy future are better in Moab. Return my daughters."

The Snake waited, not quite sure how to attack. He watched Ruth and Orpah. He thought about their names, closely allied to their natures, and how he would exploit the situation. Ruth meant "friendship" and Orpah "stubbornness." He decided to concentrate on Pleasure, now Bitterness, and stubborn Orpah, trusting she would live up to her name.

He loved in-law situations. All down the years he would be working hard turning in-laws into out-laws! He would be slithering around Bitterness and Stubbornness, for they were his kind of people. Friendship he would treat with respect, but whenever he could find a bitter mother-in-law (and he didn't have to search too far), he usually could find a stubborn daughter-in-law to match.

He watched it work again with Naomi and Orpah. Soon she would kiss her mother-in-law and go her own way. Hadn't she always? Her action would betray her physical gesture of affection. No journey together, no growth in common trial, no effort to even walk in the same direction any more. Stubbornness was too stubborn and Bitterness was too bitter to make any more effort.

Is that what it's like with you? Take heed to the lesson of Scripture. We know not the end of Orpah, but Ruth's name and fame and blessing are known around the world today.

Being far too obsessed with his work in Orpah's heart, the Snake turned around in horror as he saw Ruth take her mother-in-law in her arms and say some dreadful words. Dreadful to him, that is, but music in heaven's ears.

"Entreat me not to leave thee, or to return from following after thee: for whither thou goest, I will go; and where thou lodgest, I will lodge: thy people shall be my people, and thy God my God: where thou diest, will I die, and there will I be buried: the LORD do so to me, and more also, if aught but death part thee and me" (Ruth 1:16,17).

"That's stupid," he screamed in Ruth's ears. "Omnipotence expects you to love your mother and father; He expects you to love your husband and even your little brats; but He doesn't expect you to love your mother-in-law! He's not that unreasonable! Be an Orpah! Sure, go ahead and kiss her — that's nice! But then go your own way!"

But Ruth didn't listen. True Friendship never does. She had set her heart *steadfastly* to go with Naomi. (And incidentally, that's just about what it takes. A steadfast determination to identify with your mother-in-law!

"Your God, my God.
Your people, my people.
Your trouble, my trouble.
Your death, my death!"

That is the language of love. Omnipotence, looking down from heaven, loved Friendship so much in that moment of time, for she mirrored the very love and identification of God for sinful man. He identified with us in all our bitter bankruptcy — in all our shattered dreams and harrowing realities.

"For where you go, I will go.
And where you live, I will live.
Your people will be My people, and your God My God.
Where you die, I will die,
And there will I be buried."

And He was. And He did — didn't He?

The Hound of Heaven leads us gently back towards the City of Bread, the promises of God, and so it was with Ruth.

She had committed herself fully to this trying relationship. Having accepted Naomi's God, He enabled her to deal with her own attitude. We are not responsible, fortunately, for the attitude of our mother-in-law. We are, however, fully responsible for our own. It takes commitment to Omnipotence who enables us to *try* and not merely *tolerate*. It's a question of a decision being made to be steadfastly "minded" about it all. If we could only live out our difficult relationships in our mind and our will, leaving our emotions severely out of the picture, it would help. "I *will* go along with her. I will minister to her needs. I will produce actions that say I love you. And I will when she won't!"

When Ruth had said the words, "There *will* I be buried," that's what she meant. "I" must be buried if we wish our out-laws to be changed into in-laws. Identification then becomes toleration in the right sense of the word.

Ruth needed toleration to accept the cultural shock and the domestic pressures of two women from different generations and backgrounds living together. She needed toleration to meet the hostility and suspicion of a strange people who had been commanded by their God to ignore and ostracize such unworthy stock as she.

Friendship identified. Friendship tried and tolerated it all. True Friendship, vertical with God and horizontal with man, began to change the one so befriended. And God's love story unfolded.

"The whole city was stirred because of them," we read. Do you want to stir a city? Forget the evangelistic campaign, the TV outreach, the Christian book or tract, the backyard Bible club, the home study so carefully prepared. All these are tools well-tried and tested and effective in their way. But listen and I'll tell you how to stir a city. Are you listening? "Love your mother-in-law! Be her friend! Try. Identify like Ruth. That will do it!"

But this was not the end of Ruth's giving. Friendship knows no end. There is no quota of loving acts that duty would decree in heavenly friendships. They needed to eat, so Ruth would work. And so she went gleaning and worked so diligently that she even refused to stop to eat. The field of workers watched. They rested, they drank, they laughed and joked, but every eye was furtively watching one supple frame bent busily and beautifully over every fallen strand of barley.

Love worked. Love worked hard. Friendship got her hands dirty, and Friendship had no time to stop to eat, for

Friendship thought of Bitterness. And in her worn and calloused hands she carried home some bread. She could have kept it for herself. She did not need to share. But Naomi could not stay bitter for long when loving Ruth shared her *all*.

All was told . . .the trials and triumphs of her day, the gift of food sore come by, the start of a relationship that stirred her heart and puzzled her somewhat.

"This man, Boaz," she asked Naomi, "who is he? He happened to come by my field. He saw me at my work. He called me to him, to his very side, and gave me food in front of all his maidens. He offered me a place and safety from his men. Who is he?"

And Naomi laughed! She said, "His name is Strength. He is a relative of mine. Now, little girl, listen to me. Obey me. Do exactly as I say, for I can see Omnipotence's smiling face at last!"

"Friendship will always find Strength," Omnipotence commented. "I will see to that!"

Now Ruth would face a choice again. Would she obey her mother-in-law in regard to her love life? Would Friendship stretch that far? We see Naomi act in love. The love of Ruth had done its changing work. Now it would be *her* turn to give. For Boaz belonged to *her*. He was *her* relative, not Ruth's. She had the prior claim. Now she would give to Ruth as Ruth had given to her.

And so Omnipotence worked it out, and Love won the day. The marriage was performed and testimony given to Friendship's life.

"Is she not better to you than *seven* sons?" the people asked Naomi.

"Yes, indeed," Naomi answered reverently. "For what son could bear a child and give it up? What son would lay it in your arms and say, 'A name for you, Naomi.

Take my child and be its nurse. It's yours!' "

"What name do you give the child?" Naomi asked.

"Obed," Boaz answered her.

"How fitting!" said Omnipotence. "My God Is King married Pleasure, and the result was Sickness and Pining. Stubborness wouldn't change a thing, but Friendship could and did. Her love changed Mara, and she became the giving one. Strength added himself to Friendship and placed in an old and bitter woman's arms the gift of Worship, for so the name Obed implies."

Worship, born into a family long ago, resulted in Omnipotence promising to write his name and his mother's in His sacred book for all the world to see. The Christ would be of Mary's line, and their names would be there.

"Even the area of in-laws and out-laws could not be fully exploited without Omnipotence's interference," fumed the Snake. He didn't believe it possible! How could Bitterness be turned to Worship?

> Omnipotence could do it,
> Omnipotence would do it,
> For Omnipotence is Omnipotence,
> And Omnipotence is strength!

Oops! I Think I've Discovered a Gift I Shouldn't Have!

Miriam

"I'm the fashion editor for a popular magazine, the vice-president of a home catalog company, mother of six, and chairman of our women's club," said a beautifully groomed modern Prime Rib. "But as far as my church is concerned, all I'm good for is pouring Kool-Aid and cutting up tuna fish sandwiches!"

The Snake rolled over and over with glee. It was true. All those talents and gifts! As long as he provided her with plenty of secular opportunity to exercise them, and as long as the church leadership continued to be so threatened by her and her gifts that they ignored them, all would be well.

The elder from the local assembly, who had been asked to visit said lady in her home and answer her awkward questions, moved uncomfortably from foot to foot.

"Well, they do need help in the nursery," he suggested hopefully.

"I can't stand squelchy, shrieking kids," she said.

"Well, maybe you could help embroider the kneelers for the prayer stools."

"Listen, sir," the lady replied, becoming increasingly frustrated, "that isn't my gift. I know I have the gifts of teaching, administration, and preaching."

"You can't have," replied the man, aghast. "You're not allowed to! God doesn't give such gifts to women!"

"Well, just who do you think I received them from?" she demanded. "The Snake?" She faced him defiantly. "Just where does it say all *that* in the Bible, anyway?"

"In Timothy . . . Paul says, 'I suffer not a woman to teach,'" answered the man triumphantly.

"Then why did he give instruction for women to cover their heads *when* they were praying and prophesying in public?" inquired the lady tartly.

The Snake was appalled. When had she read *that?* he wondered. He had no idea she had been studying the subject. He usually made sure the Prime Ribs who were gifted by Omnipotence were directed away from such dangerous passages of Scripture. "Keep them in the Martha and Mary bits," he advised his hosts of demons. Also, 1 Peter 3 is good (even though its's really speaking to women married to non-Christians). As they read through their Bibles, throw a dim light on verses like Mark 16:11, where Mary Magdalene tries to teach the disciples that Jesus had risen from the dead, and the Bible says "they believed not!" Tell them men won't believe women teachers because it's not scriptural to listen to them.

Well, the elder left the lady's house shaking his head over all this women's lib stuff. Why she'd refused the offer to teach first graders *and* arrange the flowers, he just couldn't imagine. Just who did she think she was?

After he had gone, the gifted Prime Rib began pacing up and down her living room talking to Omnipotence.

A Gift I Shouldn't Have!

Now, that wasn't good at all, the Snake decided. He tried to keep her so angry at the church leadership that she just wouldn't pray. But it didn't work. The whole situation became exceedingly dangerous.

"Omnipotence, am I wrong?" she asked. "Did You gift me to use my talents for the world or for You? I *know* I can speak well. Am I then to spend my life selling cosmetics . . . *or* selling Christ?"

Omnipotence was just about to answer when the Snake thought of a neat idea. He *had* to stop her from being turned to Paul's writings! He knew as well as Omnipotence that Paul had lots to say about a woman's gifts and the freedom to exercise such, and he had no intention of letting her get into all that.

"Why don't you start *right at the beginning of your Bible?*" he suggested. "Then work your way through, looking for things to back you up. Surely if God had intended women to be leaders in the church, He wouldn't wait until the New Testament to tell them!"

That made sense to the lady, so she began to read. The Snake curled and knotted his long evil body in black mirth and retired to his bed for a rest. He'd been especially busy the last four hundred years, and he knew it must be safe to take a breather, having directed the lady to the Old Testament. Not that his knowledge of the Old Testament Scriptures was such that he could afford to be complacent. He just knew the women in those times were treated little better than cattle, and even Omnipotence's chosen people, who should have known better, recited a little prayer before the day began. It went something like this: "I thank thee, God, I am not a Gentile, I am not a slave, I am not a woman!" No, the personhood of the Rib had not been vindicated in Old Testament days! He could afford to sleep for a little while.

111

Omnipotence laughed gently. Sitting down by the lady's side, he turned the pages of her Bible until she arrived at the Book of Exodus, chapter one.

"Let me introduce you to Miriam," He said. "See her standing by the river, having placed her little brother among the crocodiles. Examine her many natural gifts evident in the story: her courage demonstrated by her not running away as the princess appears; her quick-mindedness in offering her own mother as nurse to the baby; her clever ability and gift of words as she persuades the princess of Egypt to listen to her *and* follow her suggestions. Here is talent indeed."

"But are talents spiritual gifts?" asked the lady.

"No," replied Omnipotence. "Natural talents are not spiritual gifts. Natural talents are given according to common grace. Many non-believers have natural talents, but no unbeliever has a spiritual gift! These are given by the Holy Spirit when He enters the human heart at conversion. He it is who gifts the believer. Talents have to do with techniques and methods dependent on natural power, and as such are a gift from God. But the Holy Spirit imparts spiritual gifts that enable My children to do not only the natural things better, but supernatural things as well."

"I feel I have some natural talents, Omnipotence," the lady said, quieting down. "I found some of them by exercising and proving them, but how can I learn if I have spiritual gifts? I think I do, but the church will not allow me the opportunity to find out."

"Read on, little lady," replied Omnipotence. "Come with me to Exodus 15 and see Miriam now. She has become a prophetess *in the church!* She is right at the top along with her brothers Moses and Aaron. She is also the choir director. And no one is objecting."

A Gift I Shouldn't Have!

"Oh, if only I could talk to her," said the lady. "If I could ask her how it all happened. Did she have to fight for her rights in a day and age when women were trampled underfoot?"

"It is not altogether a question of rights or roles," said Omnipotence. "It's a question of gifts. Israel recognized her gift. Acknowledging and confirming her spiritual abilities, they held her in the same respect as Aaron and Moses. Her gift led her out of her cultural role, you see.

"I say in My Word," Omnipotence continued, "that the Holy Spirit imparts grace with the gift. The word *grace* means 'charm.' It will be a wonderfully 'charming' thing when you find a way to let the church 'see' in action the gift I have given you. People will be delighted."

"But my church isn't thrilled or delighted."

"You need to take the opportunities they open up to you," counseled Omnipotence. "If all they will allow you to do is teach first grade, then teach first grade. Prove your gift to them. If you have the gift of teaching, you can teach little children as well as adults. Start there with what you are allowed to do. Let your gift become a blessing to the little ones. Then the little ones will tell their parents, and the parents will acknowledge and confirm your charming gift exercised among their precious children. The noise of their approval will break upon the leadership's ears, and they will invite you to 'come up higher.' You have to prove yourself a blessing, not a nuisance! I will do the rest for you. Prime Ribs I placed in the history pages of time, were those who did not demand their rightful place, but allowed Me to place them in My sphere of service."

"But the men in my church seem so threatened," the lady objected. "And I know I don't help. I try to talk about it all, but then we begin to argue, and I get horribly aggressive and domineering!"

"Look at Moses," said Omnipotence. "He was not threatened by Miriam's gifts. But then there was not in all the earth a man as humble as he. Many men need to grow in humility. Under Moses' leadership, Miriam exercised her gift beautifully. She had the ability to prophesy — which means to proclaim a divine message — with results! She declared that which could not be known by natural means. And, oh, how gracefully she did it! What a blessing she became to the whole Israelite nation, and how they loved her — men and women alike."

"Was it always so?" inquired the lady.

"No," replied Omnipotence. "Just once toward the end of her life she usurped Moses' authority — the authority I had invested in him. She chose to rebuke his decision to marry the Ethiopian woman. Together with Aaron she began to 'fight for her rights,' instead of resting in my position for her. 'Has the Lord spoken by Moses only?' she demanded. 'Has He not also spoken by Aaron and me?' For this I struck from heaven, and she became a leper."

The lady gasped. "So great a punishment, Omnipotence?"

"To usurp Moses' authority was to usurp mine!" returned Omnipotence. "I simply removed her from her position of usefulness and service. She was driven outside the camp in shame. But see, Israel did not travel until she was restored to them again. They needed her, and I needed her. I would not let them journey on without her. But we could do without her pride and arrogance. She had to learn that her God-given talents and gifts must be used freely and to the full *under* the authority I had placed over her. In this case, the man Moses."

"So, there *is* a place for women?" the lady asked hopefully.

A Gift I Shouldn't Have!

Omnipotence laughed. "Read on, little Prime Rib," He said. "Come with Me to Huldah's story."

"Who's she?" asked the lady, who had honestly never heard of her.

"She's another prophetess of Mine," responded Omnipotence. "She lived in the university quarter of the city of Jerusalem in the days of godly King Josiah. She was the lady the priests of My temple and the others of My land — Yes, even the king of My country — turned to for advice when they discovered the dusty book of the law in the rubble of My temple. They needed a word of encouragement from God. I sent them to Huldah and gave them a message of hope through her lips."

"Well, that was good," replied the lady, a little doubtfully.

"But what has it to do with our talk?" asked Omnipotence, reading her thoughts. "I'll tell you. Standing by King Josiah's side was Jeremiah the prophet, My 'man of men.' But in that moment of national extremity I sent My people to Huldah, my 'woman of women'! I can speak to a nation through a woman with just as much authority and power as through a man, if I so choose."

"That's where it's at!" the lady almost shouted. "If only I could know it's Your *will* to use me."

"Come to the Gospels," said Omnipotence. "Gabriel invited a woman to make room for My Son in *her* body. I could just as easily have presented a ready-formed child to a man! A woman was first at My cradle, last at My cross, first at My tomb, and first to be told of My resurrection. They were quicker to believe than My disciples!

"Anna, old and worn, was used to speak for Jesus to all who lived at Jerusalem. What place did women have in My Son's life and ministry and in My kingdom? A large and roomy place."

Prime Rib and Apple

"But there's still Paul," the lady said.

It was now far into the night. The Snake, sensing all was not well, was awakened from his varied nightmares. To his horror, he saw Omnipotence directing the lady to Paul's epistles.

"No, no!" he shouted. "Not Galatians! Try Corinthians and Timothy. Please, please not Galatians!"

They ignored him, and Omnipotence read loudly and clearly from Galatians 3:28: "[In Christ] there is neither Jew nor Greek, there is neither bond nor free, there is neither male nor female."

"So," explained Omnipotence, "all Paul's commands to those in Christ are commands to women as well as men. Why don't we do a study of those commands first and measure your obedience, before we take two statements completely out of context and allow the Snake to shut your mouth for the rest of your life?" And so they did.

The Snake was panic-stricken. Hearing Omnipotence's beautiful voice reading the Scriptures was torture enough, but to see the light of liberation dawning in the lady's eyes was worse!

Omnipotence started with a quotation from the Old Testament, one that the Snake had successfully hidden for decades. "The Lord gives the word [of power]; the women who bear and publish (the news) are a great host" (Ps. 68:11, Amplified Bible). He then went straight to Romans 10:13-15 and read through it.

> For whosoever shall call upon the name of the Lord shall be saved. How then shall they call on him in whom they have not believed? and how shall they believe in him of whom they have not heard? and how shall they hear without a preacher? And how shall they preach, except they be sent? as it is written, How beautiful are the feet of them that preach the gospel of peace, and bring glad tidings of good things!

A Gift I Shouldn't Have!

Then He turned to 2 Corinthians 5:9,10:

Wherefore we labour, that, whether present or absent, we may be accepted of him. For we must all appear before the judgment seat of Christ; that every one may receive the things done in his body, according to that he hath done, whether it be good or bad.

He reminded the lady that she had a primary responsibility to Him. It was He she must stand before to give account of gifts used or abused while on earth.

He took her next to 1 Corinthians 12:28, which says: "And God hath set some in the church, first apostles, secondarily prophets, thirdly teachers, after that miracles, then gifts of healings, helps, governments, diversities of tongues." And He pointed out that if she was a teacher, then *He* had set her in His body as such, and it was stupid to be used as something else.

Approaching the dreaded verse in 1 Corinthians — 14:34 — that she had had quoted to her so often, He pointed out that when the men in authority did not permit a woman to speak, she was to be obedient and not to cause dissension. By the same token, if she was commanded to speak, she should also be obedient.

The problem had been partly a cultural thing in the Corinthian church. Paul had actually given great emancipation to New Testament women. Never before had they been allowed to speak in a public gathering. They had not even been allowed to teach their own children at home. Practically none were educated. But in Christ, all was changed. Each member of the body of Christ was "sexless" as far as God was concerned. Sex ceased to matter unless a girl had the gift of preaching or teaching, and then it was to be exercised under the authority of the church body. In fact, the leadership's responsibility was to help and enable each member, whatever sex, to discover his or her gift and exercise it under their control, that the whole body might be edified. In Corinth, however, this new freedom had gone straight to some Prime Ribs' heads, and they had leaped the barriers of centuries that commanded, among other things, that women worship in another part of the building and were actually shouting out questions in the worship service. Hence Paul's rebuke, "Let your women keep silence in the churches: for it is not permitted unto them to speak; but they are commanded to be under obedience, as also saith the law. And if they will learn any thing, let them ask their husbands at home: for it is a shame for women to speak in the church."

Omnipotence then took the lady to meet Phoebe, a favorite Prime Rib of His. (The Snake had always detested that girl.) Paul listed her among the leaders of the church at Rome, and so she was. The precious letter of Romans that had to be carried hundreds of miles from Corinth to Rome was entrusted to her, a mere woman. This was a job usually given only to specially trained men couriers. (Her courage sickened the Snake.) Her position in the early church was one of patroness or lawyer to the group of believers.

The lady looked long and hard down the list of leaders in Romans 16. Eight were women! Prisca, too, rose from the page of scripture to add her voice to those of Philip's four daughters, all of whom prophesied! Prisca it was who corrected the great Apollos's teaching, his doctrine needing added truth. She supplied it. She and her husband Aquila were apparently dear colaborers with the Apostle Paul.

Then there was Apphia, Philemon's wife. Euodias and Syntyche, teachers there in Philippi, and Lydia, called by Paul, "one who labored by my side."

"Now, put all this beside Paul's strange commandment not to let a woman teach," said Omnipotence. "In

A Gift I Shouldn't Have!

Timothy the case was such that the women were usurping the man's authority and therefore needed disciplining. But Paul's encompassing commitment to the gospel forced him generally to give responsibility to the most capable person, regardless of sex."

The study over, Omnipotence closed His book. The lady's eyes were shining, and she thanked Him for directing her to truth that set her free. Free to dedicate her natural talents to her Lord. Free to choose to use her gifts within the church body anywhere they would let her. Free to wait for Omnipotence's time to give her opportunities. And free to start right now with opportunities given and available.

Lifting the phone, she called the elder of her church, who was rather surprised to hear from her.

"I'd like to teach those first graders," she said quietly. The man was glad and grateful. He was tired of trying to draft people into the Lord's service. He was also glad she had found her place. He thanked her and accepted her offer. Putting the phone down, he turned around to find Omnipotence standing there.

"Now it's your turn," Omnipotence said. "Let's get My book out and start examining the whole subject, laying aside all your cultural ideas. And, oh, yes — about the little gifted Prime Rib you've just been talking to. She really can do more than pour your Kool-Aid and cut up your sandwiches! Let's see just how you can help her discover and exercise her gifts, and so edify the body . . . under your leadership, of course."

"But, Omnipotence," he protested, "she thinks she has a speaking gift. She thinks she can preach!"

"She can," Omnipotence replied. "I gifted her. She is one of My gifts to your assembly. Now what are you going to do about it? Accept or reject My gift?"

Prime Rib and Apple

The lady prayed hard for the elder and for her own attitude as well. Oh, how she longed for Omnipotence to use her. He had promised her He would. She began to dare to believe it would be so! She believed —

> Omnipotence could do it,
> Omnipotence would do it,
> For Omnipotence is Omnipotence,
> And Omnipotence is the giver of gifts.

How to Cope With Loneliness
The Little Widow

Loneliness was lonely! He decided he had to get busy *at once* and find someone with whom to share his awful state. He had been looking in the death column in the local newspaper and decided to visit the young widow down the street. Coming to the little house on a small hill, he knocked at the door. A young woman answered his summons, her tear-streaked, frantic face telling him he'd arrived at the right place.

"How would you like to live with me?" he inquired with a lonely smile.

"I don't want to live with Loneliness!" she cried, slamming the door in his face. "Go away. Go away. Oh, please, go away!" she whispered pitifully, leaning against the door.

Loneliness pouted. Then he settled down on the doorstep. He knew it would be just a matter of time before she would have no alternative but to let him in. He liked to present himself immediately to a new widow, adding to her stricken feelings and cashing in on the shock. Why did these Prime Ribs believe they were immortal, he wondered? Why did they never allow themselves to think of widowhood? Their refusal to face the reality of the possibility helped the Snake greatly in the hours immediately after the event. As long as they continued to say "Not me" instead of "Not yet,"all was in his favor. If he had been able to feel sorry for her, he would. But Loneliness only feels sorry for himself, so he contented himself with watching the proceedings through the keyhole.

The young lady was talking to her two small boys. She'd talk a little, cry, put her arms around them and hold them close. Then, setting them away from her, she would talk some more.

It was certainly difficult for her, Loneliness observed. I mean, just how *do* you tell your children they are about to be taken away as slaves to pay for last weeks' groceries?

Loneliness noticed they were all sitting on the floor. That's strange, he thought! Peering through the window, which gave him a much better view than the small keyhole, he saw that the entire house was absolutely empty. Not a stick of furniture remained. There was nothing in the house! He had heard she had had to sell everything she possessed to pay her bills, but had not realized "everything" meant "everything"!

Suddenly he was jogged out of his reverie by the opening of the little lady's front door. Where was she going? She had left her two children behind and was hastily making her way through the village to a small house on the outskirts of the compound. He followed.

"Oh, no!" he thought, as he recognized the name on the "scroll" box. *Elisha lives here*, it said. He noticed that the wretched box was simply stuffed with messages from Omnipotence. That was enough in itself to keep Loneliness away. He could never survive around the commands and promises of God! To his great consternation, the little widow was welcomed into the prophet's house and began to pour out her complaint to Omnipotence's friend.

Now, to be a friend of Omnipotence meant *never* to be alone. For this reason, Loneliness had never had a chance to get to know Elisha. The air around the man was often overcrowded with horrid angels. In fact, he usually didn't go anywhere without the entire seventh army of heaven escorting and protecting him! No, Elisha was definitely an enemy to be reckoned with.

Sneaking inside the door, he listened apprehensively to the ensuing conversation. It started off in quite an encouraging way. The little widow began by questioning Omnipotence's good judgment. She recounted how unfair she felt it all was, when her dear husband had loved and served Omnipotence so well. He had even given everything up to be trained as a full-time prophet! She was angry.

"Well, now," thought Loneliness. "That's very good." She was angry at Omnipotence, and now she was angry at Elisha. She was going to be very angry at the creditors who were coming to take away her children, and she was certainly angry at him! (That didn't seem quite fair, he thought. After all, he was the only one offering her any sort of constant companionship.)

Anyway, he certainly was pleased to see her angry. That would lead to heavy guilt feelings about her anger, which would all contribute to a growing depression. Feeling things were going well, he slipped out of the house. Actually he was glad to go, as the *Presence* was so overpowering everywhere. Loneliness knew his survival depended on the absence of the Presence!

Elisha looked with great compassion on the little lady. "What can I do for you?" he asked, so very gently. How his heart broke for her. Her husband had been an outstanding young man, close to the old prophet's heart, and he had had his own hard questions when one so young and vibrant had been so tragically struck down.

"You must love him *very* much, Omnipotence," he had said when he had been brought the news of the young man's death. "You couldn't do one moment more without him! How special he must be to You to take him to Yourself so soon!" No, there was no problem rejoicing in the young prophet's sudden release into *life* in the presence of his beloved Omnipotence; the problem was the crumpled face and anguished eyes of the lovely young girl facing him. Desperate with the responsibility she was no longer able to fulfill, angry at Omnipotence, and helpless to stop her beloved children from being torn from her side, he watched her cast herself at his feet.

He prayed silently to Omnipotence. "Father, help me! Give me Your compassion and understanding. Help me to listen long, and allow her to unburden her agony. Keep me quiet in loving sympathy until she is finished with her complaint. Help me show her that to be angry at death, as You are angry at death, is not wrong. But help her, Omnipotence, not to be angry at You, who are her only source of real help."

So he prayed, and so she wept. Then the tears stopped. Looking into the prophet's eyes, she knew he cared. She knew she was loved. He would tell her what to do. He would give her hope instead of despair. He would help her to trust Omnipotence again.

"What do you have in the house?" the prophet asked

her after the torrent of words had ceased and they were seated at the table.

"Nothing," she replied. "Absolutely nothing! Nothing to sell, nothing to eat, nothing to burn on the fire, nothing to sleep on. Nothing! I have borrowed from my neighbors and my friends, but now they want their money, and I have none. The people are harsh and cruel. They care not. They just want to be paid!"

"Think, little Prime Rib," the prophet urged. "Are you sure there's nothing in the house?"

"Just a little pot of oil," she replied.

Elisha smiled. "Forgotten in plenty, remembered in your poverty. Omnipotence's provision has been there all the time!" he murmured. The little widow gazed at him wonderingly, and Elisha began to explain what she must do.

Meanwhile, back at the widow's house, Loneliness was glad to see that the moving van had arrived with his furniture. He didn't have much, but he wanted to get it all in place before the little lady returned from her visit with Elisha. The children objected to him intruding into their mother's life, but he rudely reminded them they had better be kind to him, as he would have them both to himself in a short time. No slave master would be able to afford two little boys, he said, so they might as well get used to his company!

He began to move his belongings into place, preparing for a long stay. He struggled through the door with his huge magnifying glass. It weighed so much, but the Snake had helped him mount it on wheels so it could quickly be placed in front of his victims. Each time a new situation would arise, the problem would be magnified out of all proportion. Loneliness does that!

Next he opened a tin of "loud silence." That always

helped to amplify his presence. Moving swiftly from room to room, he scattered it in every direction. The only place he couldn't get it to stick was the area around the little boys!

Next he set his big clock on the mantlepiece. Adjusting it carefully, he smiled with approval as it began to tick away. Every minute was twice as long as a real one, and the hands were specially weighted so they appeared never to move at all. Loneliness always makes time drag!

Having distributed the magnifying glass, clock, and contents of the tin of silence, Loneliness decided it was time to call in a member of his family — a son of his named, appropriately, Super Sensitivity. It was a bit difficult getting him to come, because he immediately attributed quite the wrong motive to Loneliness for asking him! He'd always been an extremely difficult child to raise, either being dissolved in tears, shrouded in silence, or enjoying a pout. However, he finally came and agreed to play his part, which would be to encourage the new widow to suspect people's motives and offers of help and to encourage her to withdraw from society more and more, until she became willing to live with Loneliness.

The stage set, Loneliness laughed a sort of lonely laugh and waited for his victim's return. He did not need to wait long. Bursting into her home, the little widow marched straight through the living room into the kitchen and began searching the shelves one by one.

"Whatever is she looking for?" Loneliness asked Super Sensitivity.

"How should I know?" snarled that prickly character, suspecting his father was accusing him of planting something in the cabinet!

"Just a little pot of oil," the widow was murmuring as she searched diligently on the dark, empty shelves. Finding it, her face lit up in almost rapturous hope. Holding it gently, she spoke to it as though it were alive. "I come to you in my poverty," she said, "as the representative of the source of my survival and the saving of my sons."

Loneliness had an immediate cardiac arrest. Omnipotence had done it again. He watched aghast as the wretched woman turned his magnifying glass upon the little pot of oil instead of on the empty house! Having been reminded by Elisha of God's real and adequate presence in her life, represented by the precious oil, she was now looking through his glass at the size of God's provision for her.

Loneliness was furious. He was not used to being used to magnify Omnipotence! Having actually used his glass, the awful woman marched over to his clock on the mantlepiece. Laughing a horrible laugh (it sounded very much like real joy), she twirled the hands around the clock face and said, "Time, you shall not drag for me any more. I'm going to make sure I am so busy serving Omnipotence and doing all the things He will give me to do that time will fly!" And with that she picked up Loneliness's clock and made it do just that — right out the door.

Glaring at Super Sensitivity, she told him she had just learned that she was only responsible for her own attitude, not for the attitudes and actions of others. Therefore, he could go. She refused to take personal umbrage any more. Understandably he took it very badly and sulked off licking his wounds and pricking himself with his prickles.

Turning to the amazed children who had watched the whole glorious turn of events, their mother began to give them orders. "We are going to reach out to our neighbors," she announced.

"Reach out?!" screeched Loneliness. "You can't do

that! Not when you've nothing to give!"

"Just a little pot of oil!" she answered firmly. "Elisha told me I must realize my divine provision and pour out of my poverty into other people's empty lives. So," she continued to her children, "run now and ask for empty vessels — get many of them!"

Omnipotence smiled in heaven and went to find the little widow's husband, who had been a bit worried about her. The man now knew what he had never known before — that one day is as a thousand years in heaven, and that as soon as he could drag his eyes away from his Savior's face and turn around, his beloved wife and boys would be with him in Omnipotence's home. Time was so fleeting from the perspective of eternity, but his concern had been that his darling, living in the perspective of time, would feel it to be so very, very long until they met again.

Omnipotence assured him she was doing beautifully and was just about to bring blessing to her entire community, which was, of course, one of the reasons he had not taken her home along with her husband. People needed to know that it was possible to lean on Omnipotence at such times and prove His enabling. Thus, they too would learn to hope.

"When you learn to pour yourself out into the empty vessels all around you and lose your own problems in seeking to 'be' the answer to theirs, then you will be able to rejoice in My fullness," Omnipotence said to the little widow, as she busily kept filling vessel after vessel that her sons brought to her.

"Is it magic, mummy?" the little boys asked wonderingly.

The little lady laughed. "It's greater than magic," she said. "I'm simply obeying the word of God, given to me by the man of God, about the provision of God, and I'm learning that the oil flows according to my faith!"

The creditors were satisfied, the neighbors were delighted, the bills were paid, and, of course, Omnipotence wonderfully provided for His bereaved children, as He always does.

Loneliness was back home in hell. It was awfully lonely, because even though there were so many people there, nobody was ever allowed to see, touch, or meet anyone else. That's what hell is all about — one big agony, one big absence of the Presence — the knowledge that other beings are seeking other beings but never finding . . . through all eternity. Loneliness shuddered. It was awful. And he ought to know.

Heaven is not so! Heaven is company. Heaven is seeing, touching, meeting, and loving others who love Him! Heaven is the Presence everywhere. And heaven can touch earth sometimes . . . like when a little widow asks Omnipotence that it might be so.

> *Omnipotence can do it,*
> *Omnipotence will do it,*
> *For Omnipotence is Omnipotence,*
> *And Omnipotence is there.*

How to Be a Light in a Dark Place

Esther

The Snake was seeing stars, and it was not a pleasing experience for him. He hated lights of any kind, but stars in particular, mainly because of Omnipotence's love for them. He knew God had set the stars in fixed places to give light on the earth; he also knew that sometimes the angels were called stars and had a special function in and out of time. Why, he could remember when God had laid the cornerstone of the earth and fastened its foundations, "when the morning stars sang together, and all the sons of God shouted for joy" (Job 38:7). The stars, physical and angelic, brought glory to Omnipotence, and that in itself was enough to cause the Snake grave displeasure.

He didn't really know what to do with them, that was the problem. They twinkled so much that every humanoid on planet earth could see them, even when they were millions of light years away! The worst thing about them was that they always pointed to Omnipotence, turning everyone's attention heavenward.

He was not to know that one would point earthward one grand, future day when heaven came down and glory filled — a manger. Yes, there was no doubt about it. Omnipotence obviously delighted in setting His wretched lights in dark places.

Omnipotence had His human stars, too. They were (and are) so much more precious to Him than physical lumps of rock — more important even than His created angelic spirits, for what angel did He lay down His life for at Calvary?

If, as Omnipotence's book tells us, He appoints the stars a place and calls them by their names, then how much more can we be certain that He designates a place for His human stars and knows *them* by name?

Yes, if there's a dark place, you can trust Omnipotence to place one of His brightest and shiniest stars right in the middle of it. But while physical stars shine by radiation from energy sources within, human stars have no ability to glow brightly; they must reflect the radiance of Omnipotence. When a human star that is cold and dead, just a lump of material, chooses to look to the Son, then he or she begins to shine with that reflected glory!

Hadassah was just such a star. Set in a dark place for "such a time as this," she shone for Omnipotence and brought about the deliverance of her people.

Hadassah, or Esther, literally means "star," and she had every intention of being a star! She believed the plan of God was to redeem lost mankind and that that divine plan concerned her nation Israel. She knew God's people must be pure amid impurity and keep themselves unspotted from the world that knew not God. The light of the star nation would shine in the darkness, and the darkness would not be able to overpower it or extinguish it.

From this special people, the Bright and Morning Star, the Messiah Himself, would come. Star believed it. She literally staked her life on these bright and enduring promises, and she trusted even when she lived "in such a time as this" — "such a time as this" being possibly one of the blackest and darkest periods of her nation's history.

Star knew that the bad situation was due to the disobedience of Omnipotence's people. But she also knew that His promises were still true or reliable. The promises of God are able to accomplish His purposes even when the Snake and man have done their worst to stop them! Heaven and earth would pass away, but His Word would not. It could not! He had promised that a remnant of her nation would be faithful, and one day the Light of the World would light up this dark place.

Now you who are reading these pages may say, "So what? I believe too!" But are you living in light and happiness? Are you surrounded by good will with an unsullied sky above you? In those circumstances it is easy to believe God's good promises to us!

But if, like Esther, you were a little slave girl in a heathen king's kitchen, possibly in chains, humbled and humiliated constantly, then you might know how hard it is to go on believing in His promised ability to keep His word! Hard it is, but possible. Esther proved it so!

She must have wondered so often about the plan of God and His promises. But this we know, she staked her life on the providence of God that would enable Him to keep His promises concerning His plan.

What happens to us when we find ourselves in the middle of dark situations? Do we believe the things that are happening to us are accidental? Do we seek to change our circumstances, or do we accept them with a fatalistic attitude? *Can* we change our circumstances, or should we even try?

Sometimes we *can* change things, and we *must* always try. That is why we are there! At other times, having tried, we find we cannot alter anything, nor can we escape, and so we must allow those situations to change us and we must accept the privilege of shining there.

Esther shone! When she found herself in the king's palace with no way of changing anything, except the beds, she accepted it with God's grace and used it all to God's great glory.

Now maybe you are like Star. You feel a slave of your circumstances, and you can't change a thing. You've tried everything you know, but now you say, "It's still awfully, awfully dark in my little piece of sky!" You need to get your feet on the bedrock of the fact that God is a size bigger than *all* of your darkness. Bigger than your chains, bigger than your captor king, whoever he is. Bigger, bigger, bigger!

Now Star had to believe in a *big* God to believe He *could* be bigger than King Xerxes! King of 127 provinces gained by burning and pitiless torture, he had become bored with his sensual orgies and offered a prize for some new indulgence with which to titillate himself! A cold, calculating despot, a mixture of passionate extremes, he made the name of Persia awe the ancient world. It was normal to have magnificent parties for months on end on his palace grounds. And Esther was his slave! She ran and served and slaved and trembled in his presence.

The Snake had enjoyed his part in her debasement. He had watched with enjoyment as her country was invaded and the soldiers killed her mother and father slowly before her eyes. He had been much annoyed at her uncle's intervention. Watching ferociously, he saw Mordecai take the child for his own, protecting her all he could on the long, exhausting march into captivity. He heard that kind and godly uncle instructing her to obey authority, even *this* new and dreadful authority, for it was Omnipotence who chose the kings of the earth, he said. Even heathen ones! He set up one and removed another according to His will, and He was in control. His children's duty was simply to obey.

Did Esther understand? She did — she shone! She did as she was told. Obeying her uncle enabled her to obey her slave master, as long as obeying the law of that authority did not contravene the specific law of Omnipotence. Esther learned to be an obedient and faithful slave.

One day as she and her fellow slaves cleaned up after another vast party in the palace, she heard angry voices in the king's chamber. Now she knew, as all the slaves knew, that the king's wife had committed an unpardonable act the night before. Commanded to appear before her master and his friends, who were quite drunk with wine, she had refused! And now her fate was being determined. She must be deposed, the councillors advised, for how could all the men of the king's realm continue to hold their manly heads high and keep control over *their* wives when news of Vashti's disobedience reached their ears! "We will find you a new and more obedient queen," they promised, and so the king agreed.

The slave quarters were abuzz with speculation. Couriers had been sent abroad to search the king's domain. There was to be the greatest beauty contest of all time. Hegai, the keeper of the women, was believed to be beside himself with all these kidnapped girls to care for. Some were proud to come, but others, torn from husband, home, or family, were no company for each other or for him! Competition, spite, and envy abounded.

When Hegai sent for slave help in the harem, Esther was among those chosen to work for him. Nearly beside himself, Hegai turned to snarl his orders at the girl who had appeared at his summons — and stopped. Star shone! Hegai commanded her to stand still as he walked slowly around her. Star's heart pounded against her ribs. How very small and alone she felt. She wanted to run away back to her dark cellar. The jealous eyes of hoards of captive beauties glared at her. What had she done wrong? Would she be whipped? She prayed, "Oh, dear Omnipotence, help me now. Help me now."

Star shone. She was ready. Perhaps she would be punished, but she didn't care. Belonging to Omnipotence, one must be ready to be punished. Mordecai had taught her so.

Hegai couldn't take his eyes off her lovely, young face. He had never seen such a face before. It was not her beauty, although she was certainly beautiful, but the strange, calm radiance about her that was different. Different from anything he had ever seen before. He commanded the keeper of the slaves to come to him, and taking the awful chains away, he set Star free. "You can join the contest," he said. "Maybe, just maybe, you might win!"

"Win what?" she asked.

"The queen's crown!" he said.

The Snake was aghast. He could see what was going to happen if he didn't make a quick move to stop it. Omnipotence was working this wretched, shiny thing into the darkest place on earth . . . the king's throne room! Well, it wasn't going to happen, not if he could help it! He'd had marvelous fun directing the king's atrocities without any of Omnipotence's light around for quite some time now, and he had a big plan afoot. He intended to move the greatest Jew-hater of all time against Omnipotence's people and wipe them out. Star would not be a help at all. She might shine into the darkness and give the game away!

Star shone on! Yes, she did. Obeying her new master, which she had been instructed and trained to do, she quickly became Hegai's favorite. What sweet submission she displayed. Hegai was so completely charmed with her that he preferred her above all the other women. He even gave her seven maidens to serve her.

A year passed, the required preparation time for the young women. Esther's day approached, and the king's bedchamber loomed large on the horizon. In the evening a girl would go to the king, and in the morning she would return to the king's harem for the rest of her life. Star trembled. Was Omnipotence greater than this? One night with Xerxes! One night in bed with him! How do you face that *and* praise the Lord? And what if she did not please him? She'd be locked away forever in his harem. Never again would she see her sweet uncle's face.

Each day faithful Uncle Mordecai walked before the house in which she lived. He asked continually for her, and servants told her of his loving questions. He was praying for her daily, continually. "Oh, Omnipotence, keep him praying," she whispered, "as the day draws near!" A sensual, heathen ogre and a little virgin Jewish girl who didn't know the ropes! She was going to need all the prayer help she could get.

And so Esther's turn came and passed. Star shone! The king, like Hegai, gazed with awe upon her radiant beauty. He loved her most of all and made her queen! Set free from that grim harem, Star was released to serve another master. Xerxes himself!

She had to believe it was no mistake on Omnipotence's part. She must submit, serve the king well, and use the situation for Him. She would be the best queen Persia had ever had! She would show them all what a difference belief in Omnipotence could make!

Her uncle cautioned her. By now he'd been promoted to the great king's council.

"Don't tell the king your origin," he said. "Wait and see what God has in mind. Xerxes could depose you from your place of influence if he finds out he wed a Jewish slave! Just serve him well and be obedient." Star obeyed, for had she not always obeyed her uncle since her childhood days?

"Oh, if all My children would learn obedience like this," Omnipotence said. "To learn to obey the authority set above them, whether it be father, mother, teacher, or king, makes it easier to learn to be obedient to *Me!*"

The Snake flicked his tail and continued on his evil way. He thought for a moment he might remove Xerxes and replace him with a worse monarch. But then he decided that would be too difficult. For one thing, he knew there *wasn't* a worse monarch around, and for another, he had *tried* to instigate two of the king's councillors to kill him and the plot had fallen through. His plans had been frustrated by that wretched Mordecai, who had discovered the plot and warned the king!

"Meddling Jew, your days are numbered," he hissed to himself. He maneuvered Haman into place.

Now Haman was one of the Snake's favorite people. He had every characteristic that showed to whom he belonged. He was of his father the devil, who was a murderer from the beginning. He hated, and that was a good start; but even better than just hating people, he hated the Jews! Now that was very good, the Snake decided happily.

142

Perhaps Haman could be encouraged to exterminate the whole race.

The Snake smiled approvingly as the king signed the entire Jewish nation's death warrant. He even looked on admiringly as the city panicked and the king and Haman sat down to drink to it.

It had really been very easy, the Snake thought. All it had taken was egotistical Haman demanding an edict for the citizens to prostrate themselves before him. Mordecai, needless to say, had declined (being willing to bow only to Omnipotence), and Haman had discovered his nationality and had decided in a fit of rage to exterminate him and his whole nation with him!

"There's a people among your subjects, your majesty," he had announced to the king, "who are not helpful to you. They are subversive and arrogant and are spreading their growing influence. I would like you for your *own* benefit to order their death and promise those who execute such to take possession of their goods and all their property. Seeing many are quite wealthy, we shall make sure it is accomplished this way!" The king nodded impatiently and signed the edict.

Mordecai was devastated. Donning sackcloth, he mourned his nation's fate. Star, hearing of his agony, ceased to shine! How could she be at peace when her beloved uncle demonstrated such distress of heart?

"Whatever is the matter?" she inquired of him through her servants. And so he told her all. Then he asked her to go in and plead for the king to save her people's lives!

Star was appalled. "I can't," she said. "It is death to appear before the king unless he sends for me, and I've been out of favor! It's been a whole long month since I have seen his face."

143

Prime Rib and Apple

"Star, little Star," Mordecai answered, "do you think you will escape when judgment falls? You are a Jew, remember! If you fail, Omnipotence will send deliverence from another place. But don't you see? God has placed you in the palace 'for such a time as this'! Was ever the sky so dark for your people as now? Yours is the privilege. Yours is the choice. He trusts you with it all."

Star prayed. Star yielded. Star sent a message to Mordecai and said, "Gather our people and fast and pray for me! I will do the same. Then I will go in to the king. And if I perish — I perish!"

So the time had come! To shine or not to shine! It must have been a great temptation not to shine. That would have meant escape from death. After all, she *was* the queen! No one need know her nationality. Surely her uncle would not tell. To shine meant almost certain death! It was the law of the Medes and the Persians that she would be contravening by presenting herself unasked before the king. It would be a greater sin than Vashti's! But *what* was the lesson she had learned as a child? She knew it well! When the law of man contravenes the law of God, she *must* act against it. Even unto death! Her nation must be saved.

She realized how important it was that she *had* been obedient until now. She knew she was a most beloved queen. If she had not been previously obedient, she would not dare seek the king's face now. Having behaved so well, maybe — just maybe — her king would extend his golden scepter to her. This was the only hope of being forgiven for such a breach of Persian law!

Having prayed and fasted, she dressed herself in her most fabulous royal robes. Walking toward the throne room of the king upon the arm of her servant, she trembled violently with great fear. The king sat in state upon his throne so very still and quiet. "If I did not do this, how could I stand before a greater throne than this?" Esther encouraged herself desperately. "Omnipotence is my Lord, not Xerxes. Maybe I shall shortly see Him face to face, and then I shall be glad!" Star shone! Yes, she did! And Omnipotence moved the king's strong hand towards his golden scepter of forgiveness. Star touched it, oh, so very thankfully! She was safe. Omnipotence had answered her prayer!

She asked the king to dine with her the next day, and he accepted her sweet invitation. Haman too was asked. Delighted, Haman told his wife, and yet his great delight was tinged with fury when he thought of Mordecai with his head held high in pride before him. To appease him, his "nice" wife suggested he spend the evening building a high gallows in the back garden so that he might seek the king's permission to hang his enemy there. The Snake chuckled with delight as it was done.

That night the king was unable to sleep. What's a king to do when he can't sleep? Well, he can count slaves or read a book, of course! A book was brought, and there the king discovered Mordecai's good deed of kindness written down — that is, how he had saved his life some time previously. He noted that Mordecai had not yet been rewarded for the deed. At that very moment, Haman came along, and the king inquired of him, "Haman, what would you do to the man the king delights to honor?"

"Who else but me?" Haman thought to himself. "Why, put him on a horse and proclaim such before him throughout the city," he replied aloud.

"Good," replied King Xerxes. "Go and do so for Mordecai the Jew!"

Heaven laughed, the Snake stood stupefied, and Esther was encouraged to give the king her request.

At dinner it was done. Casting herself down at her master's feet, the queen pled, "Save my life, O master king!"

"Who dares to threaten *you?*" the king demanded.

"This wicked Haman," she replied.

The king in rage went out into the garden, and Haman cast himself upon the queen's couch to plead for his life.

Returning to the room, the king thought he was trying to rape the queen, and so Haman was dispatched to die upon the very gallows he had built for Mordecai!

The queen's request was granted. Salvation for the Jews! Their enemies were destroyed, and Mordecai was elevated to the position that Haman had held — prime minister of the empire!

Many years later when Star arrived in heaven, Omnipotence talked to her about it all. He said how much her story would encourage others down the years. Many little Prime Ribs would undergo the tests she'd known. Many "slaves" of circumstances would shine for Him, believing He had placed them there to do so. The Holy Spirit would be like Mordecai — with them all the time, daily coming to see how they fared, refusing to bow to Haman who represented the Snake. He would be the One who would encourage those little stars to speak or to stay silent, even as Mordecai had so instructed her. The dreaded Haman would not be able to hurt the stars, for they belonged to the King, and power belonged to the King! Over and over again as Haman sought the life of those who sought to shine, there would be one brave star who would dare to enter in before the King on their behalf. The Golden Scepter would extend from heaven's throne that they should not be consumed by His power. The King would gladly grant them their request. "The Golden Scepter is a picture of My Son," He said. "He it is whom the stars may touch and so come near My throne!"

"I shall destroy the Snake one day," Omnipotence concluded. "But until that time, I'll be placing My shining ones in dark places and giving them a choice! Shine for Me, I'll ask them — just as I asked you."

Star shone brightly near her heavenly Master. At last she served a King whose service was her perfect freedom! How eternally glad she was that she had made the choice to shine! What warmth and joy was hers forever! "Shine, little stars," she whispered into the dark world.

> *Omnipotence will help you,*
> *Omnipotence shall use you,*
> *For Omnipotence is Omnipotence,*
> *And Omnipotence is light!*

Prime Rib and Glory

"Come back soon, Son," said the Father.

"I will, Father," replied the Son. "In thirty-three years!"

"Your throne will be waiting for You," said Omnipotence very quietly.

Heaven hushed as Omnipotence instructed a small angel to wrap up the Glory His Son was laying aside. "Place it tidily under the throne for an interval, till Calvary is over and My Son comes home again," He said.

The angels gathered round to say good-by, telling Him they would be caring for Him while He lived on earth. They would be there at Bethlehem, Egypt, later in the wilderness, and, of course, Gethsemane! "And we'll *all* be at Calvary!" they shouted. "Ten thousand times ten thousand of us!"

Gabriel came near and cast himself at the Son's feet. "I have told the small and highly favored Prime Rib You

151

will be coming," he said. "She welcomes You."

The Son smiled. "Thank you, all my ministering spirits," He replied.

The small angel came near his favorite Person. "Where are You going when You leave home?" he murmured. "To Bethlehem?"

"No," answered the Son.

"To Nazareth? Or Galilee? To the Mount of Olives? Or Calvary?" he inquired, his eyes widening as each question brought a softly spoken negative from the Son.

The little angel dared ask no more. He was so sure he had heard someone say the Son was going to Calvary! He was all confused and upset. He looked helplessly at Omnipotence, who was looking at His Son in the strangest way. The third member of the family, the Holy Spirit, stood there, too. All three members of the Godhead just stood quietly, looking at each other! Somehow the little angel knew that the most stupendous thing that had ever happened in eternity was about to take place.

The choir was assembling, practicing their new music: "Glory to God in the highest, and on earth peace, good will toward men."

Why, the heavenly ink was hardly dry, the small angel noticed. Was the choir leaving as well, he wondered? Did *they* know where the Son was going? "Oh," he agonized, "I would give a few worlds to know the answer to *that* question!"

As if He had read his angel mind, which of course He did, Omnipotence took a heavenly moment from contemplating man's redemption to give His little ministering spirit an answer.

"My Son is *not* going to Bethlehem, Nazareth, and Calvary," He explained. "He is on the way *to His throne!*"

The choir burst into a rapturous rendering of a "Hallelujah" chorus, only to quiet like a fading sunset as they saw the Father's face. He had opened heaven's door, and the Holy Spirit was already hovering over a Prime Rib's fifteen-year-old body.

"Go to my fallen friend, My Son," Omnipotence said. "Be born King, to live a King, to die a King, to rise a King. Your *throne* awaits You!"

The King didn't answer, for He was lying in His human mother's arms. He was no longer than eighteen inches, naked and helpless, bound in swathing bands, tied down quite securely! He was utterly dependent, which He had *never* been before!

The little angel couldn't see all this, of course; besides which, a very embarrassing thing had just happened to him. As Omnipotence had opened the door of heaven for the choir, he had inadvertently tumbled out into the heavenly places. It was pretty dark after gloryland, and at first he kept bumping into clouds. (Well, he was only in second grade, remember!) However, he quickly found himself at earth's surface, and hastily putting on his heavenly brakes (the large oak did help a bit), he began at once to search for his King.

Coming upon Caesar's palace in Rome, he felt sure the King would be there, but the man in charge *obviously* wasn't Jesus. Next he flew to Jerusalem to Herod's palace, but he soon learned that the man in charge was a usurper and didn't even belong to the royal line.

Suddenly he became aware of a shadowy form beside him — the Snake! "Goodness me," he thought aghast, "didn't the Father lock him up? Whatever was the great adversary doing loose at a time like this?"

"I'm looking for the King, too," said the Snake, answering his angel thoughts. "Not that I'm really bothered about finding Him," he continued craftily. "I've many kings that belong to me who are far more glorious than He!''

The little angel remembered that Omnipotence had told all His ministering spirits they were *not* to argue with the Snake, as that was how the whole mess had started in the first place. They were supposed to let Father God rebuke him. But the little angel loved the King so well that he *had* to say something! He felt himself getting *very, very hot!* He'd never felt so hot and twinkly in all his life. He didn't know the sensation that was burning him up was called *righteous anger.*

Well, here was this slimy thing telling him that these moth-eaten human creatures in fancy pants with tin lids on their heads were greater than *his King!* Fortunately for him, the Holy Spirit suddenly appeared and placed the little angel safely behind Him.

"Kings there may be," He told the Snake, "but none *born* King. What king of earth is a king *before* his birth?"

The Snake howled with rage and fled away to search for heaven's gift so cleverly disguised, and the small angel found himself deposited gently back in heaven, where he most definitely belonged for a few more million years!

Omnipotence found him carefully rewrapping the Glory all over again! He was longing, as only an adoring angel can, for a sense of Him, a touch of Him. He couldn't see very well. "Dear me," he thought, "I've caught the humans' tear disease."

Now this was quite serious, as angels have eyes all over them, so he was becoming very wet indeed! The Father went to fetch His heavenly handkerchief that He keeps in heaven to wipe away all tears off all faces.

"What's the matter, little spirit?" He asked ever so gently.

"How could Omnipotence take time out to be so kind with all that He has on His mind?" wondered the small angel.

"You love My Son," replied the Father simply.

"Where *is* He, Omnipotence? Please tell me!"

"Come with Me, and I'll show you," the Father said. "I sent Him in disguise, lest Snake, cruel man, or jealous monarchs should find Him. I wrapped Him up in human baby form and laid Him in the hay, for *who* would think to search for God in heaps of smelly straw?"

He pointed to Bethlehem and His most blessed of all Prime Ribs, explaining,

> *Mary had within her human frame the God who made her.*
> *Sheltered in a dirty cave, gave birth to Him who loved her!*

The little angel gasped! *His King.* Helpless. Absolutely helpless. Unable even to tell the rebel world how much He loved it! Well! If He couldn't speak for Himself for a little while, he knew someone else who could! Yours truly!

He thanked the Father and rushed away to the heavenly stores to look for some really meaningful Christmas cards to send to earth. He picked up one, put down another. They didn't seem quite right. Then he found just the thing. "It's a boy," it said. He bought a few million and ordered a special-issue heavenly stamp, a "Bi-Billion-Tennial" one. He was lining up some cherubs, who needed occupying, to address them to the "kings of the earth and their subjects," when Omnipotence came by and told him softly, "No! Not that way!"

The small angel showed Father God the card: "Mr. God would like to announce the arrival of a Son. 8 lbs. 6 oz. Name: King of Kings and Lord of Lords."

But Omnipotence shook His eternal head and went His way.

Deflated, the little angel sat down to think. He *had* to do something. Maybe the King would like him to bring a little piece of the Glory down to His manger for Him, to make Him feel more at home! Quietly snapping off a little piece, he sneaked out a heavenly window, following a late choir member down to earth. (You thought there wouldn't be any of *those* in heaven, didn't you?) The trouble was that the choir angel was millions of years older than he, and he just couldn't keep up. He ended up exhausted, sitting on a high cloud from whence he had a fantastic view of the King and the whole world. The little piece of Glory that he carried illuminated him so beautifully that he became the very brightest and best object in the skies!

Gazing at his King, he could contain himself no longer. *He told! Yes, he did!* Pointing, too, which was really *very rude!* He decided he would be on the safe side and tell some men thousands of miles away, men of another culture, country, and religion. And so he did. But then, oh, how his angel smile faded. Well, how was he to know they would almost swallow their telescopes and follow him?

He tried to shake them off, but every time he looked back over his pointer, there they were. He hid the Glory in his pocket and disappeared over Jerusalem, because he knew he musn't give the game away to Herod. But when he peeped from behind a cloud, to his horror he heard them quizzing everyone.

Boy, was his star *red* when they spilled the beans. The inhabitants of Jerusalem weren't the only ones who were troubled!

The little angel gazed anxiously at the King and saw

Him smile. Whew, it was all right then! He suddenly remembered Father God had always liked enthusiasm. In fact, that's how creation happened. It was Omnipotence being enthusiastic!

"What *did* the small King know?" wondered the angel, as he lovingly tucked the Glory around the little form and watched it light the faces of the adoring shepherds. Maybe the Father would let him stay around and care for the Son in His growing years.

And so the years passed and the Son went about His Father's heavenly business — He lived to die for you and me. And the Father raised Him from the dead and said to man, "You have done your worst — now I will do *my best!* I care not what *you* think of Him. This is what *I* think of Him; I place Him on His throne! *Exalted,* here He *reigns* in heaven, *King of Kings and Lord of Lords!"*

Can you guess who was first on the portals of heaven to welcome Him back from Calvary? That's right, the little angel! He'd been clapping his wings so hard that they were very sore, and now the Father instructed him to place the Glory around the Son. And so he did, but in so doing found the strangest thing. To his great consternation, he discovered he had some left over! How could this be? What had gone wrong?

He stood there in front of heaven's throngs, feeling so unbelievably silly, until he heard the Son say to the Father, "O Father, glorify thou me with thine own self with the glory which I had with thee before the world was. . . . And the glory which thou gavest me I *have given them.* . . . Father, I will that they also, whom thou hast given me, be with me where I am; that they may behold my glory" (John 17:5,22,24).

So *that* was it. The Glory he had left was for those who were to believe in the Son and put their trust in Him. The little angel watched them come from every country through the ages and heard them praise his King ... Prime Rib and Adam, Little Dripping Tap and Job, Abraham and Sarah, David and Bathsheba, Ruth, Hannah, and Naomi, transformed and conformed to the image of the Son. As the little angel carefully placed the Son's Glory around them, he exclaimed with delight at the finished result. They were singing a song and thanking the Son for coming to their earth to redeem them. The small angel, who could never know the joy of redemption, listened wonderingly to the words of praise.

As we stand before Your throne,
Dressed in beauty not our own,
As we gaze at Christ in Glory,
Looking on life's finished story,
Now, Omnipotence, we know –
Not till now – how much we owe.

Then the little angel understood "Why Christmas?" And with all of heaven and earth, he glorified the King.